NEURO-LINGUISTIC PROGRAMMING

Using NLP, dark psychology, mind control, psychological warfare, and CBT (cognitive behavioral therapy) to learn how to manage your emotions, influence people, and the effective use of persuasion, manipulation, and deception.

By

Michael Charles

TABLE OF CONTENTS

INTRODUCTION

The idea of neuro-linguistic programs has pulled in a lot of research lately, particularly in connection to discourse generation. It is apparent, for instance, that the mind doesn't give engine directions each fragment in turn. At the point when we consider the entire scope of components that influence the planning of discourse occasions, (for example, breathing rate, the development, and coordination of the articulators, the beginning of vocal-overlap vibration, the area of stress, and the position and span of stops), a profoundly complex control framework must be utilized; generally, discourse would deteriorate into a sporadic, disrupted arrangement of commotions. It is currently perceived that numerous zones of the cerebrum are included: specifically, the cerebellum and thalamus are known to help the cortex in practicing this control. In any case, it isn't yet conceivable to build a definite model of neurolinguistics activity that considers all discourse generation factors.

Envision how enormous your mind is and its numerous experiences with various musings daily. Your cerebrum is deciding on a breakdown regardless of whether you don't care for it when it has arrived at its point of confinement. Irrespective of whether confirmations or reactions are being stated, our cerebrums hold it. The main contrast is reactions will, in general, last more and incenses our regard. It seriously influences our presentation in our everyday lives, and subsequently, we fall flat. Every single one of us experience adrenaline surge when you like something and that adrenaline belittling when somebody said you are bad enough — some endeavor to be better yet a few tumbles down together with their desire. Word is an amazing asset that we can utilize, either to elevate or crash our very own and another person's soul. On and when yours has been slammed down, right now is an ideal opportunity to recover it. As far as Neurolinguistics, the main utilization of language is to imbue constructive considerations into an individual's brain.

CHAPTER ONE

WHAT IS NEURO-LINGUISTICS?

Neurolinguistics is the investigation of the neural components in the human mind that control the cognizance, creation and obtaining of language. As an interdisciplinary field, neurolinguistics draws techniques and speculations from fields, for example, neuroscience, semantics, subjective science, correspondence issue, and neuropsychology. Analysts are attracted to the field from an assortment of foundations, bringing along a variety of trial procedures just as broadly fluctuating hypothetical points of view. Much work in neurolinguistics is educated by models in psycholinguistics and hypothetical phonetics and is centered around exploring how the mind can execute the procedures that hypothetical and psycholinguistics propose are essential in creating and understanding language. Neurolinguists study the physiological components by which the cerebrum forms data identified with language, and assess phonetic and psycholinguistic hypotheses, utilizing aphasiology, mind imaging, electrophysiology, and PC demonstrating.

Neurolinguistics is generally established in the improvement in the nineteenth century of aphasiology, the investigation of phonetic shortfalls (aphasias) happening as the consequence of mind harm. Aphasiology endeavors to connect the structure to work by dissecting the impact of mental wounds on language preparation. One of the principal individuals to draw an association between a specific mind territory and language preparing was Paul Broca, a French specialist who directed post-mortem examinations on various people who had talking lacks, and found that a large portion of them had cerebrum harm (or sores) on the left frontal projection, in a zone currently known as Broca's zone. Phrenologists had made the case in the mid-nineteenth century that diverse mind areas did various capacities and that language was for the most part constrained by the frontal districts of the cerebrum, yet Broca's examination was perhaps the first to offer exact proof for such a relationship, and has been portrayed as "age making" and "vital" to the fields of neurolinguistics and intellectual science. Afterward, Carl Wernicke, after whom Wernicke's region is named, suggested that various territories of the cerebrum were specific for various phonetic errands, with Broca's region dealing with the engine creation of discourse, and Wernicke's territory taking care of sound-related discourse perception. The field of aphasiology and the possibility that language can be contemplated by looking at the physical qualities of the cerebrum. Early work in aphasiology likewise profited by the mid-twentieth-century work of Korbinian Brodmann, who "mapped" the outside of the mind, splitting it into numbered territories dependent on every region's cytoarchitecture (cell structure) and capacity; these zones, known as Brodmann regions, are still broadly utilized in neuroscience today.

The begetting of the expression "neurolinguistics" is ascribed to Edith Crowell Trager, Henri Hecaen and Alexandr Luria, in the late 1940s and 1950s; Luria's book "Issues in Neurolinguistics" is likely the primary book with Neurolinguistics in the title. Harry Whitaker promoted neurolinguistics in the United States during the 1970s, establishing the diary "Cerebrum and Language" in 1974.

Despite the fact that aphasiology is the verifiable center of neurolinguistics, as of late the field has widened impressively, thanks to a limited extent to the development of new mind imaging advancements, (for example, PET and fMRI) and time-touchy electrophysiological strategies (EEG and MEG), which can feature examples of cerebrum enactment as individuals take part in different language assignments; electrophysiological systems, specifically, rose as a feasible strategy for the investigation of language in 1980 with the disclosure of the N400, a cerebrum reaction demonstrated to be delicate to semantic issues in language cognizance. The N400 was the main language-applicable occasion related potential to be recognized, and since its revelation, EEG and MEG have gotten progressively broadly utilized for directing language inquire about.

Communication with different fields

Neurolinguistics is firmly identified with the field of psycholinguistics, which looks to explain the intellectual systems of language by utilizing the customary strategies of exploratory brain science; today, psycholinguistic and neurolinguistic hypotheses frequently advise each other, and there is a lot of cooperation between the two fields.

Much work in neurolinguistics includes testing and assessing speculations set forth by psycholinguists and hypothetical language specialists. As a rule, hypothetical etymologists propose models to clarify the structure of language, and how language data is sorted out, psycholinguists propose models and calculations to clarify how language data is handled in the brain, and neurolinguists break down mind movement to surmise how organic structures (populaces and systems of neurons) complete those psycholinguistic preparing calculations. For instance, tests in sentence preparing have utilized the ELAN, N400, and P600 mind reactions to analyze how physiological cerebrum reactions mirror the different expectations of sentence handling models set forth by psycholinguists, "sequential" model, and Theo Vosse and Gerard Kempen's "unification model." Neurolinguists can likewise make new expectations about the structure and association of language-dependent on bits of knowledge about the physiology of the cerebrum, by "summing up from the information on neurological structures to language structure." Neurolinguistics inquire about is readiness in all the significant territories of semantics; the fundamental etymological subfields, and how neurolinguistics tends to them, are given in the table underneath.

The Interdisciplinary Nature of Neurolinguistics

Which controls must be considered in neurolinguistics? Mind and Language express that its interdisciplinary center incorporates the fields of etymology, neuroanatomy, nervous system science, neurophysiology, theory, brain research, psychiatry, discourse pathology, and software engineering. These controls might be the ones generally associated with neurolinguistics; however, a few different orders are likewise profoundly significant, having added to speculations, strategies, and discoveries in neurolinguistics. They incorporate neurobiology, humanities, science, psychological science, and computerized reasoning. In this way, the humanities, and medicinal, common, and sociologies, just as innovation, are spoken to altogether.

Co-advancement of Language and the Brain

It is uncontroversial, in logical circles in any event, that the human mind has experienced rapid development in late advancement. The cerebrum has multiplied in size in under one million years. The reason for this 'runaway' development (Wills, 1993) involves guess and interminable discussion. A solid case can be made that the extension of the cerebrum was an outcome of the improvement of communicated in language and the endurance advantage that having a language presents. The territories of the mind that experienced the most noticeable improvement have all the earmarks of being explicitly connected with language: the frontal flaps and the intersection of the parietal, occipital, and worldly projections.

Neurolinguistics and Research in Speech Production

The idea of neuro-linguistic programs has pulled in a lot of research as of late, particularly in connection to discourse creation. It is apparent, for instance, that the cerebrum doesn't give engine directions each portion in turn. At the point when we consider the entire scope of variables that influence the planning of discourse occasions, (for example, breathing rate, the development, and coordination of the articulators, the beginning of vocal-crease vibration, the area of stress, and the position and span of stops), a profoundly refined control framework must be utilized; generally, discourse would decline into an inconsistent, disordered arrangement of commotions. It is currently perceived that numerous zones of the cerebrum are included: specifically, the cerebellum and thalamus are known to help the cortex in practicing this control. In any case, it isn't yet conceivable to build a definite model of neurolinguistic activity that considers all discourse generation factors.

Envision how enormous your cerebrum is and its numerous experiences with various musings daily. Your cerebrum is choosing a breakdown regardless of whether you don't care for it when it has arrived at its farthest point. Irrespective of whether confirmations or reactions are being stated, our minds hold it. The main contrast is reactions will, in general last more and infuriates our regard. It seriously influences our presentation in our everyday lives, and thus, we fall flat. Every single one of us experience adrenaline surge when you like something and that adrenaline censuring when somebody said you are bad enough — some endeavor to be better, yet a few tumbles down together with their aspiration. Word is an incredible asset that we can utilize, either to elevate or crash our own and another person's soul. If yours has been smashed down, this is the ideal opportunity to recapture it. Regarding Neurolinguistic, the main utilization of language is to imbue constructive contemplations into an individual's brain.

Neurolinguistic means to change the plan of an individual's conduct. It could assist an individual with making out of his/her potential and show to the world that he or she can take on anything. Essentially, the extent of the program is to ponder the individual's conduct and reinvent it through reaching the mind. This sort of approach is once in a while called the "study of greatness" due to suitable treatment for primary issues, for example, fears, issues, and preferences. These issues hinder the development of an individual as it were that they are reluctant to go past their usual range of familiarity. By investigating, you can find yourself and your restrictions; that is the reason you truly need to peel off that area of you that is terrified.

On and when you consider looking at Neurolinguistic, it will open you up in the realm of Amazement. It is unquestionably the harmony that you want. Envision. No fears or disarranges so implies opportunity. Opportunity to dream, find, and accomplish. Your assurance emerges because your certainty is helped. You can become whoever you need to be and get anything you desire to have. In that sense, you can call it flawless life.

Try not to block yourself. Be bold and play. Since you have control of what you can turn into.

If you need to enable your brain to liberate it based on what is confining it inside since it is such a great amount of better to live outside your safe place, there are things yet to find, love yet to give, and individuals yet to meet. On and when you are apprehensive, that is ordinary yet search out for ways that can give you a chance to live better, since you merit it. We all merit it. On and when you believe that the past is frustrating you, desert it since the future is a lot of significant than the past. It is something that is intended for us to design, decide, and accomplish. So put out your peddle and sketch your future above all, you have to liberate yourself based on what is keeping you down.

Neurolinguistics, the investigation of the neurological systems basic the capacity and handling of language. Although it has been decently agreeably discovered that the language focus is on the left side of the equator of the mind in right-gave individuals, debate remains concerning whether singular parts of language correspond with various specific regions of the cerebrum. One sort of research carried on in this field is the investigation of aphasia, a state of the cerebrum where language capacity is disabled or devastated. Brief aphasia has been incited by electrically animating the cortex of cognizant patients to decide the area of the different elements of language. Albeit exceptionally broad focuses of language have been proposed, it appears that there are no profoundly specific focuses. A few cases have been accounted for of patients who, in the wake of having their left side of the equator of the mind expelled, adjusted in the correct half of the globe the language work that the left side of the equator had. When all is said in done, nonetheless; however, progress is being made in this field, next to no is known for sure about the neurological parts of the language.

CHAPTER TWO

WHAT IS NEURO-LINGUISTIC PROGRAMMING (NLP)?

NLP is the act of seeing how individuals compose their reasoning, feeling, language, and conduct to deliver the outcomes they do. NLP furnishes individuals with a system to display remarkable exhibitions accomplished by prodigies and pioneers in their field. NLP is additionally utilized for self-improvement and achievement in business

A key component of NLP is that we structure our one of a kind inside mental maps of the world as a result of how we channel and see data retained through our five faculties from our general surroundings.

Neuro

Every individual has set up their own special mental separating framework for handling a great many bits of information being assimilated through the faculties. Our first mental guide of the world is comprised of interior pictures, sounds, material mindfulness, inward sensations, tastes, and scents that shape as a consequence of the neurological sifting process. The main mental guide is called 'First Access' in NLP.

Semantic

We, at that point, dole out close to home importance to the data being gotten from the world outside. We structure our second mental guide by doling out language to the inside pictures, sounds, and sentiments, tastes, and scents, therefore, framing regular cognizant mindfulness. The second mental guide is known as the Linguistic Map (at times known as Linguistic Representation)

Programming

The conduct reaction that happens because of neurological sifting forms and the resulting etymological guide.

Richard Bandler and John Grinder created neurolinguistic Programming (NLP) in 1975. Neuro identifies with the cerebrum and the manners by which we process data from our five detects. Phonetic identifies with language or correspondence, and how we use images to compose and offer significance to our encounters, how we speak to our encounters in our inner world. Programming alludes to how we code our encounters and program our subliminal with practices, channels, convictions, and so forth. On and when we were PCs, NLP would be the investigation of our programming, and these things that make up our elucidation of life and decide our encounters. It's exceptionally emotional. Every one of us has our projects, the vast majority of which were found out at a very young age. Since it endeavors to see how we do what we do, it likewise uncovers the methods for changing or reconstructing our subliminal. It enables us to comprehend brain science in a manner that is anything but difficult to apply to day by day life.

Essential suppositions of NLP:

The guide isn't the region. Representation is at the core of NLP. Your involvement with the world depends on your observation, not what is genuine.

Experience has a structure. How we experience the world, channel, and example reality and how we code things into our psyches are organized. When you see how somebody structures their world, you can assist them with making changes. Changes to the structure will bring about another experience.

There is no disappointment, just input. You can't generally do anything incorrectly. We're all testing and discovering what works for us and what doesn't. Each experience gives you input that enables you to move what you're doing, in the long run, giving you the outcomes you need.

The importance of correspondence is the reaction it gets. On and when you are speaking with somebody, attempting to express what is on your mind, the importance is controlled by the audience, not the talker. Regardless of how you state it, the message the audience gets depends on how they translate it. It really is great to consider who you're conversing with and how they decipher their reality if you truly need to get your significance crosswise over to them

If what you're doing doesn't work, accomplish something other than what's expected. NLP is about adaptability. Too often, we continue saying very similar things to ourselves, and playing out similar practices, yet anticipate that things should change. All change starts inside.

The individual with the most adaptability has the most power in a circumstance. Living stuck gives you the groove's eye to see.

You can't NOT impart. You're continually speaking with your voice, your eyes, your signals, your vitality. In any event, saying nothing has meaning. You have every one of the assets you have to accomplish your ideal result. It's simply a question of arranging them unexpectedly.

Each conduct has a positive goal. All practices are the aftereffect of your intuitive, attempting to accomplish something positive for you. Individuals proceed with negative behavior patterns for one reason; there is a reward included. Regardless of whether there are practices that you don't care for, the aim behind them is certain. It is conceivable to accomplish a similar positive expectation with another, progressively attractive conduct.

The mind and body and interlinked and influence one another. Contemplations make feelings, feelings change our bodies down to the sub-atomic structure. Your inner discourse is leading the entire show.

Individuals are substantially more than their conduct. You can adore somebody sincerely, a kid, for example, dislike their conduct. The kid isn't 'awful' the conduct is. Having a decision is superior to not having decision. Try not to get tied up with an injured individual mindset. You generally have a decision. Demonstrating fruitful execution prompts greatness. If another person can do it, you can do it. You can figure out how to display greatness by focusing on how specialists do it - how would they think, feel, inhales, what are their qualities and convictions.

NLP is something that you see best once you begin to utilize it. All things considered, you are your very own research facility. You can search inside and perceive your considerations, the pictures you make, the sensations you feel, investigate how your convictions constrain you, and what could occur on, and when you transformed them. NLP gives its clients numerous systems and apparatuses for personal growth, constructive change, and self-awareness. You can do a significant number of techniques on yourself and start evolving today. Working with a professional is unquestionably simpler; however, as a prepared master can see things we don't enable ourselves to see. In any case, you can change, and you can change quickly with NLP.

NLP (the abbreviation for Neurolinguistic writing computer programs) is a self-awareness situated methodology completely investigating every human response and communications to inward or outside improvements. NLP intrigue centers around unlimited potential outcomes of emotionally encountering an everyday reality. A similar aptitude or capacity is distinctively created because of individual experience; hence, people should discover advantageous intends to interrelate, convey, and coordinate. Modifying our sensorial mindfulness while interrelating and mingling, we may effortlessly see those noteworthy enhancements rise out of a progressively adaptable way to deal with a genuine world.

A constructive rebuilding of individual observations may change your everyday life. For example, cutoff times are bad dreams for everybody, you can't leave each time you feel under strain, and certainly, you can't change time passing. Possibly you should search for the appropriate response inside, hence, attempt first to coordinate your qualities with specific necessities inside your profession ventures. Before long, you'll see that things are truly showing signs of improvement, and you may feel urged to continue. Nothing has changed except for an alternate methodology of a similar issue when you diversely coordinated your perspective, acting, and communicating.

On a similar reason for individual methodology, as in the previously mentioned model, NLP works proficiently with correspondence.

Correspondence depends fundamentally on a pre-setup set of shows and a typical multicultural foundation. Ambiguities and mistaken assumptions are inadequacies of significant social associations; in this way, NLP distinguishes the satisfactory methods through the misuse of every single human sense (for both speaker and audience) for a proficient correspondence grouping. At the point when you send or get a message, you actuate by methods for sensorial mindfulness various ideas, and consequently, you prevail with regards to relegating sense to your message. Because of an individual or abstract discernment, at least two people come to build up a typical coding.

Neurolinguistic programming incorporates a wide range of procedures that license specialists to reevaluate their observations effectively. Also, specialists, experts, and chiefly patients profit by these assorted remedial varieties because each individual methodology life in his particular manner and ordinarily reacts better to a specific methodology. As indicated by specialists' contemplations, NLP methodologies are contrastingly deciphered and named. For example, a few advisors approach NLP as an upgrading strategy for our qualities, and different authorities take them for renovating or corrections systems.

It merits referencing that meta-programs, meta-reflect, hypnotherapy, self-hypnosis, or care are very mainstream procedures as they have helped numerous individuals recapture their inward harmony. Although the relationship of terms and ideas (Neuro, semantics, and programming) may appear to be modern, it rearranges how we adapt to everyday difficulties. Also, it prompts an essential end. Incredibly, we are no different yet entirely unexpected.

NLP represents Neuro-Linguistic Programming. Neuro alludes to your nervous system science; Linguistic alludes to language; programming alludes to how that neural language capacities. In the end, Learning NLP resembles learning the language of your psyche!

We should make this easier with a model.

Have you at any point attempted to speak with somebody who didn't communicate in your language, and they couldn't get you? The exemplary case of this is the point at which somebody goes out to a café in a Foreign nation, and they think they requested steak; however, when the nourishment appears, it turns out they really requested liver stew.

This is the sort of relationship that the majority of us have with our oblivious personality. We may think we are "requesting up" more cash, a happy, solid relationship, harmony with our relatives, and having the option to adhere to a healthy eating regimen... yet except if that is the thing that appearing, at that point, something is presumably becoming mixed up in interpretation.

In NLP, we have an adage: the cognizant personality is the objective setter, and the oblivious personality is the objective getter. Your oblivious personality isn't out to get you; rather, it's out to get for you anything you desire throughout everyday life. Be that as it may, if you don't have the foggiest idea how to convey what you need appropriately, it will continue bringing steaming bowls of liver stew out of the kitchen.

Actually, proceed at present and consider if there would be one thing you could transform, one propensity you could break, what might it be?

- Would you resist the urge to panic during work introductions?
- Quit tarrying and investing such a great amount of energy on Facebook?
- Not eat up an entire pack of potato chips or tub of frozen yogurt in one sitting?

Whatever it is, understand that your oblivious personality does that since it imagines, that is the thing that you need. ("Sir, here is your lingering alongside a side of tension. I've likewise advised the valet to raise your psychological weight according to your solicitation. Will you need something else?")

Neuro-Linguistic Programming resembles a client's manual for the cerebrum, and taking an NLP preparing resembles figuring out how to get conversant in the language of your psyche so that the supportive "server" that is your oblivious will at long last comprehend what you truly desire.

NLP is simply the investigation of astounding correspondence both with yourself and with others. It was created by demonstrating astounding communicators and advisors who got results with their customers. NLP is a lot of devices and methods; however, it is far beyond that. It is a frame of mind and a technique of realizing how to accomplish your objectives and get results.

NLP Training

At the point when the NLP engineers started to share their insight, NLP Certification got accessible with different mentors. Thirty years after the NLP origin, cutting edge NLP preparing comes in all shapes and sizes, some brilliant, some great, a ton of normal, and some distinctly poor. At the NLP Academy, we are glad for our preparation record. The nature of NLP Academy Practitioners and Master Practitioners says a lot for our work.

We are pleased with every one of the individuals who graduate with the NLP Academy and attempt to help their future advancement. With the arrival of the NLPedia Study Sets, we remain solitary as the main organization in the UK, offering veritable multi-tactile home learning bundles that help the quickened learning NLP accreditation courses.

NLP Application

An NLP Practitioner can utilize his/her abilities as a specialist of progress working with people, gatherings, or organizations, or even worldwide associations and governments. As an innovation, NLP has a stunning reputation for actuating a quick and proficient change in people and gatherings.

Numerous individuals study NLP to assist them with getting increasingly powerful in their picked field. The examples can be utilized over a wide region of utilizations extending from fields as assorted as training, group building, deals, advertising, self-improvement, authority, and instructing. Any place there is human collaboration and development potential, NLP can be utilized to create and improve execution.

So what began with a wanton interest regarding how virtuosos played out their enchantment, has now developed into a global field of NLP Trainers, Practitioners, and individuals exceeding expectations because of applying Neuro-Linguistic Programming in their callings and individual lives.

NLP currently includes in more than 1000 instructive books on subjects going from master NLP matters, brain research, deals, arrangement, the executives, child-rearing, and quickened learning. There are a large number of NLP open workshops around the world, preparing more than 20,000 individuals every year across the globe facilitated by pro-NLP Trainers.

Most of the value business classes will currently incorporate parts of NLP, which likens to a figure of a huge number of individuals figuring out how to utilize NLP, and that figure is developing each year.

NLP Modeling

Coding examples of virtuoso

The examples of any virtuoso can be duplicated through demonstrating.

NLP Training

The preparation of NLP designing

- NLP Practitioner

- NLP Advanced Tools

- NLP Master Practitioner

- NLP Trainers Certification

Neurolinguistic writing computer programs is an elective way to deal with psychotherapy and is a relational correspondence model that was made during the 1970s.

Another approach to portraying it is the investigation of the structure of the subject's understanding and what can be determined from it and is predicated upon the conviction that all conduct has some structure.

It is hard to clarify precisely what it is because the etymologists and the mathematician who thought of it were keen on a few things: fruitful individuals, brain science, language, and PC programming. The individuals who began this and the individuals who are were engaged with this utilized dubious and uncertain language saying Neurolinguistic programming implies various things to various individuals.

Since the models that comprise NLP portrays how the person's mind capacities, they are utilized to educate them, along these lines, it's anything but symptomatic apparatus. It must be applied and in this manner, educated tentatively.

Many methods do not educate them, anyway they are instructed by the establishment from a well-prepared Neuro-Linguistic Programmer.

One topic keeps re-happening in the definition is it helped individuals change by instructing them to program their cerebrums. We're told that we were given the minds, yet not the guidance manuals and Neurolinguistic writing computer programs are the guidance manual for the cerebrum.

Neurolinguistic programming depends vigorously, either subliminally or intentionally, on three things, one - the idea of the oblivious personality as a continually impacting cognizant idea and activity and two figurative discourse and conduct, particularly expanding on Freud's translation of dreams and third hypnotherapy.

The essential standard of Neurolinguistic writing computer programs is that the words we use in ordinary language, mirrors an entomb, intuitive understanding of our issues. On and when these words and recognitions are mixed up, as long as we keep on utilizing them and consider them, the fundamental issue will endure. As it were our demeanors are, it might be said, an inevitable outcome.

A great association in NLP can be comprehended as far as a few significant stages, including building up compatibility, gathering data about an issue mental state and wanted objectives, utilizing explicit devices and procedures to make mediations, and incorporating proposed changes into the customer's life. The non-verbal reactions of the customer guide the whole procedure. The first is the demonstration of building up and keeping up compatibility between the professional and the customer which is accomplished through pacing and driving the verbal (e.g., tangible predicates and catchphrases) and non-verbal conduct (e.g., coordinating and reflecting non-verbal conduct, or reacting to eye developments) of the customer.

When affinity is set up, the professional may assemble data (e.g., utilizing the Meta-Model inquiries) concerning the customer's present state just as help the customer characterize an ideal state or objective for the connection. The professional gives specific consideration to the verbal and non-verbal reactions as the customer characterizes the present state and wanted state and any "assets" that might be required to overcome any issues. The customer is commonly urged to think about the results of the ideal result, and how they may influence their own or expert life and connections, considering any positive expectations of any issues that may emerge (for example, biological check). Fourth, the professional helps the customer in accomplishing the ideal results by utilizing certain devices and procedures to change inside portrayals and reactions to improvements on the planet. At last, the progressions are "future paced" by helping the customer to practice and coordinate the progressions into their life rationally. For instance, the customer might be approached to "step into the future" and speak to (rationally observe, hear, and feel) what it resembles having just accomplished the result.

Psychotherapeutic

Early books about NLP had a psychotherapeutic center, given that the early models were psychotherapists. As a way to deal with psychotherapy, NLP has comparable center suppositions and establishments in the same way as some contemporary brief and fundamental practices, for example, arrangement centered brief treatment. NLP has additionally been recognized as having impacted these practices with its reframing procedures, which look to accomplish conduct change by moving its specific circumstance or significance, for instance, by finding the positive implication of an idea or conduct.

The two fundamental remedial employments of NLP are: (1) as an extra by specialists rehearsing in other helpful controls; (2) as a particular treatment called Neurolinguistic Psychotherapy which is perceived by the United Kingdom Council for Psychotherapy with accreditation administered from the outset by the Association for Neuro-Linguistic Programming and all the more as of late by its girl association the Neuro-Linguistic Psychotherapy and Counseling

Association. Neither Neuro-Linguistic Programming nor Neuro-Linguistic Psychotherapy is NICE-affirmed.

NLP is a fix every one of that treats an expansive scope of physical and states of mind and learning troubles, including epilepsy, nearsightedness, and dyslexia. With its vows to fix schizophrenia, wretchedness and Post Traumatic Stress Disorder and its rejection of mental diseases as psychosomatic, NLP imparts likenesses to Scientology and the Citizens Commission on Human Rights (CCHR). There is little proof that NLP intercessions improve wellbeing related outcomes.] to rehash NLP, NLP isn't generally a firm treatment yet a ragbag of various methods without an especially clear hypothetical basis...[and its] proof base is practically non-existent. NLP gives off an impression of being a shallow and gimmicky way to deal with managing psychological wellness issues. Tragically, NLP has all the earmarks of being the first in a long queue of mass promoting classes that imply for all intents and purposes fix any psychological disorder...it gives the idea that NLP has no observational or logical help with regards to the fundamental principles of its hypothesis or clinical adequacy. What remains is a mass-advertised serving of psychopablum.

The clinical therapist addresses the estimation of the NLP adage—a presupposition in NLP language—there is no disappointment, just input". The refusal of the presence of disappointment reduces its educational worth. Three instances of unambiguous recognized individual disappointment that filled in as a catalyst to incredible achievement. As indicated by Briers, it was "the bite, the dust sort of disappointment, not the cleaned NLP Failure Lite, for example, the disappointment that-isn't generally disappointment kind of disappointment" that pushed these people to progress. Adherence to the adage prompts self-expostulation; the individual undertaking is a result of contributed esteems and desires and the expulsion of by and by noteworthy disappointment as minor input successfully slanders what one quality. Now and then, we have to acknowledge and grieve the demise we had always wanted, not simply coolly expel them as irrelevant. NLP's reframe throws us into the job of a single man maintaining a strategic distance from the torment of sadness by jump frogging into a bounce-back association with a more youthful lady, never stopping to express a legitimate farewell to his dead spouse. The NLP saying is narcissistic, conceited, and separated from thoughts of good duty.

Neurolinguistic Programming and Metaphors

These days, NLP specialists utilize illustrations and narrating strategies as they give a satisfactory way to fruitful direction in self-improvement programs. Generally, neurolinguistic programming representations are relative methodologies utilized to set up a successful correspondence with your obviousness. Also, these similitudes based procedures urge people to become innovativeness centered people. A specific circumstance, particularly a troublesome one, maybe anticipated into an absolute diverse light with the goal that the subject encounters effectively in any event one brilliant minute. Allegory put together methods depend principally concerning inventiveness and creative mind forms and on the capacity to interface keenly various ideas and thoughts.

Neurolinguistic programming allegories have an incredible effect on examination with understood saying. These procedures are more than a semantic apparatus; they actuate both oblivious and cognizant sides, utilizing components that have a well-characterized worth or importance for someone in particular inside a particular setting. For example, current instructive methodologies urge instructors and teachers to modify themes they should educate kids or youngsters' circles of intrigue. Along these lines, they are progressively compelling in keeping them centered. What's more, this rearrangement system to another arrangement of qualities improves the correspondence level as the message is passed on as indicated by the recipient 's (decoder) individual qualities. Generally, an individual could respond distinctively to a similar snippet of data when the message is firmly associated with the positive or negative aspect of life.

Neurolinguistic programming representations ought not to be considered controlling methodologies since they are essentially applied when we need to prompt positive reasoning.

An illustration is a portrayal utilized for clarifying an idea as far as some other idea. It usually causes us to comprehend something that isn't usually known regarding something that we know about. An illustration is subsequently a signification as far as some other thing. For instance, when we state, "Her face was as pink as a rose," it demonstrates how ruddy her face looked. Since we realize how a rose looks, we can identify with it and better comprehend the idea of the face. A similitude additionally gives an alternate point of view of conduct or a circumstance. Illustrations are incredible assets utilized in Neuro-semantic programming for compelling correspondence.

Straightforward and Complex Metaphors

In Neuro-etymological programming, similitudes incorporate analogies, metaphors, jokes, stories, illustrations, and purposeful anecdotes. Allegories can be utilized to improve correspondence just as take care of issues. According to Neuro-etymological courses, an analogy, as a rule, offers quickness to the discussion, and can make realistic and vital pictures in the psyche. An illustration can rouse or demotivate an individual since it leaves an enduring picture in the brain.

Whenever utilized appropriately, it can help accomplish a powerful correspondence or result.

There are a few basic analogies or metaphors; however, the greater part of them has become banalities. This is because they were defined a long time back, and are never again noteworthy or remain constant. For instance, the allegory 'As white as a sheet' started when just white sheets were accessible everywhere throughout the world. On present occasions, this announcement won't have the equivalent figurative power, and younger ages won't have the option to identify with them or handle their significance. Such similitudes or prosaisms are not adequate to those uninformed of its criticalness. Consequently, it is fitting to utilize such allegories simply after thinking about the group of spectators, and focusing on the ideal result.

Neuro-semantic programming likewise incorporates complex illustrations, for example, stories, purposeful anecdotes, and analogies. This sort of similitude animates the brain of the audience by including stories that have the profundity of significance and character. These similitudes are not implied for passing on explicit data, yet rather opening the psyche of the audience and opening new entryways. These analogies get to the oblivious personality and can reveal concealed issues. Since a story connects typically with the psyche in vacation mode, the cognizant personality isn't alarmed, and unwanted legitimization or analysis can be maintained a strategic distance from.

These methods can be mastered by utilizing Neuro-semantic preparing.

In a few Neuro-etymological courses, representations are utilized for initiating a stupor or speaking with an individual in a daze. In Neuro-semantic preparing, allegories can be used to incite inventiveness and take care of knotty issues. They are utilized in ordinary discussions for passing on a thought without culpable somebody or imparting threatening vibe.

According to Neuro-phonetic programming, allegories can animate the correct side of the cerebrum. They start comprehensive reasoning and animate the creative mind by utilizing visual and tactile pictures. You can picture, hear, and feel the analogy, and along these lines, help become a significant connection in the Neuro-phonetic mental guide. By utilizing these tangible rich words, we can all the more likely comprehend a thought or idea. Our oblivious personality, for the most part, makes a connection between any new data and the broad database put away inside. Illustrations go about as an impetus for making this Neuro-semantic association.

Numerous famous evangelists and educators have utilized straightforward stories as a method for conveying significant facts. Master Neuro-phonetic communicators, pioneers, and moderators have utilized analogies for a rousing, affecting, and inspiring individuals. Narrating is a significant method for learning in certain societies, and illustrations have motivated a few innovations also. Utilizing allegories is a workmanship, and can be gotten from the hang of utilizing Neuro-semantic preparing.

Utilization of NLP Metaphors in Communication

There are a few systems given in Neuro-etymological courses for utilizing representations in correspondence. These Neuro-etymological techniques are:

1) Simplifying

According to Neuro-phonetic programming, a solitary representation can pass on significant importance by being both a productive and compelling specialized apparatus. That implies the allegory is brief, exact, and creates the ideal result. A similitude is rearranging when it utilizes a recognizable idea to pass on the importance and make an interior interface. These disentangling illustrations go about as a scaffold between complex components and are utilized by a few Neuro-semantic communicators.

2) Depersonalizing

Representations can be utilized to keep away from legitimately culpable or humiliating somebody in a discussion, yet passing on the planned significance. This should be possible by utilizing a theoretical circumstance or a story where no close to home remarks are made. In this way, a suitable message can be separated by a group of spectators without feeling scrutinized or pointed at. Since the instinctual protection component isn't dynamic in a story, it is simpler to show an alternative perspective to an individual who might not have typically acknowledged any change.

3) Stimulating Creativity

According to Neuro-semantic courses, analogies are related to the correct cerebrum. Representations can get to the oblivious personality, and in this manner, help draw out the inventive energies of an individual. By titillating the inventive side, an individual can be progressively open to various arrangements, and his inward assets can help take care of any issues. These analogies are predominantly used to plant a thought or sustain a shrouded quality of the brain. These allegories can achieve remarkable advancement and inventiveness and were normally utilized by Einstein to enter the imaginative mode.

4) Enlightening

According to Neuro-etymological preparing, the illustrations we use in our language demonstrate what we are. For instance, a few people may utilize similitudes on cash. These individuals, as a rule, are cash disapproved or business arranged. By tuning in to the representations that we or others use, we can come to know the qualities behind them. This data can be then used to build up compatibility and convey viably utilizing coordinating methods.

5) Matching

This strategy can be utilized to at first match the estimations of the other individual utilizing a story, and afterward, present another idea or method for getting things done by changing the closure. For this situation, you are pacing somebody's experience utilizing an allegory, and afterward driving them to acknowledge another choice.

6) Personalizing

According to Neuro-semantic courses, this procedure is especially helpful in associations. An association, all in all, can have the picture of being an indifferent, apathetic substance. In such a case, it is required to customize the allegories and advance to the human conclusions, as opposed to talking as far as legitimate and non-individual language. Representations are generally used to place life in the association and speak to the organization's crucial culture.

7) Getting consideration

Analogies are utilized to stand out and hold the degree of focus. Our mind likes to tune in to stories, tales, tales enhanced with special visualizations and tactile language. We wind up engaged and, once in a while, get exhausted with these sorts of representations. On and when you cautiously watch an alluring and engaging speaker, you will find that his discourse is loaded up with allegories. The data passed on along these lines will likewise remain longer in memory.

8) Overcoming obstruction

According to Neuro-semantic preparing, allegories are incredible methods for keeping away from clashes or opposition. You can pass on an issue as far as a story, and ask the individual with the issue to end it. Since no immediate blame dealing is included, the appropriate response can turn out as the completion.

9) Creating distinctive recollections

Illustrations make a visual, sound, and sensation picture in our inside psyches. They carry life to the correspondence, and we can see, hear, and feel the thought being moved — this outcome in enlisting the thought solidly in our minds and recalling that it long after the discussion.

10) Insight and thoughtfulness

A similitude is additionally a contemplation apparatus for self-improvement. By getting to the correct cerebrum, you can take advantage of the oblivious personality and discover answers to inquiries on yourself. You can likewise pick up understanding about the other individual, by distinguishing the illustrations utilized.

11) Identifying issues

Analogies can find issues. The arrangement of an issue isn't as significant as recognizing the issue itself. By utilizing analogies as stories or tales, concealed issues can surface. At the point when you become deliberately mindful of an issue, you would then be able to discover the arrangement.

12) Generating feeling

Analogies contact our feelings and sentiments, utilizing tangible frameworks. A short story loaded up with certified sentiments can make us chuckle or cry, something that a non-figurative piece can't accomplish. Our conduct depends on our feelings and is utilized to settle on choices and take activities. Successful communicators, in this way, know the significance of utilizing the human creative mind and drawing in the heart rather than the cerebrum.

Neurolinguistic Programming and Fast Phobia Treatment

Neurolinguistic programming prescribes a quick solution for treating various fears, a kind of self-arranged treatment that requires the subject to somewhat disengaging himself from a phobic encounter. This healing technique depends on a controlled and incited separation from any danger. The multiplied separation stage happens just into a sheltered domain where the subject finds a way to dissect his reactions to phobic improvements equitably.

The entire experience occurs as indicated by a pre-built up situation where the individual effectively imagines applicable occasions of a phobic encounter. As a rule, some outside components are utilized to turn as sensible as conceivable the normal projection. The individual experiencing fear is approached to envision that he is sitting in the first line of a film corridor; at that point, he is required to enter the projection and as yet staying on the seat (twofold separation).

Rehashed projections, in high contrast, or hued show, in reverse and advance perceptions, are the primary strategies to enable the individual to confront his internal feelings of dread slowly. Bit by bit, the individual deserts negative feelings of dread as he is increasingly more presented to phobic occasions. On this rule, the patient is picking up bit by bit full control of his sentiments and recognitions. Boosts that before reproduced phobic occasions, don't have any longer a similar effect, by one way or another they have lost earlier noteworthiness or the essential image that was recently appointed to them.

NLP (Neurolinguistic Programming) firmly underpins people to completely investigate their inward power while battling different passionate issues dependent on their enthusiastic qualities.

What is Neurolinguistic Programming and How Does it Work?

Neurolinguistic programing-NLP-is one of a kind union of brain research, trance, phonetics, and computer science. Fundamentally, it offers specific procedures and techniques to build individual viability. In recent years, a huge number of individuals worldwide had the option to utilize the standards and procedures of NLP to change their conduct and results, simultaneously impacting other individuals.

How precisely would we be able to accomplish the ideal outcomes? We have every one of the assets we have to change our conduct; we should simply to discover the individual (or people) who have just done what we need to accomplish. To distinguish models of greatness and utilize similar techniques they utilized. Everything began as an investigation of the connection between nervous system science, etymology, and examples (models) of conduct (programs).

NLP demonstrates to be amazingly helpful and simple to utilize apparatus for the individuals who are worried about their personal development and improvement. The adequacy of this new model of life originates from the way that it very well may be received and utilized by anybody.

Neuro-phonetic writing computer programs are a hypothesis of language, correspondence, and considerations related to a helpful strategy, which guarantees that individuals can improve their method for associating with the world by rehearsing certain procedures. These systems enable individuals to improve their lives. Fundamentally, NLP assigns a frame of mind of interest, enthusiasm, and commitment towards the investigation of human conduct.

NLP was immediately advanced as a type of mental treatment, which tends to an assortment of issues including fears, sorrow, social issue, psychosomatic ailments, and so on. Afterward, it was advanced as a "study of greatness," which investigates how fruitful individuals from various zones of action get splendid outcomes.

The fundamental reason of NLP is that the words we use to mirror an internal, intuitive impression of our issues. A significant number of NLP's apparatuses and applications are utilized in treatment, business, the board, and training.

Self-awareness and explicitly neurolinguistic programming ideas depend on the following declaration it's everything up to you". Any individual can create and rebuild his life as long as he finds the best approach to control productively past encounters. The key is to initiate positive, drawing in and motivating recollections that can get underway effective new companies. Recollections utilize every human sense, so on, and when you recognize a happy memory, you will induce a bigger setting since that memory isn't disengaged. In actuality, that feeling is firmly identified with various outer and inward upgrades. We can make our future more splendid on and when we attempt to interface positive and inspiring arrangements of our past with the present and future activities.

It is a specialists' undertaking to uncover the best possible strategy and the most proficient procedures to approach the following day of our life diversely. Right off the bat, we should abandon every negative perspective, a kind of separation, and recall solely glad occurrences. This strategy fills in as an activity you should rehearse ordinary, a kind of self-change by positive parameters. NLP Specialists prompt "students" to begin their training with common unsophisticated activities of their everyday lives, and once they have procured the method appropriately and the outcomes are apparent, they should feel urged to expand the zone of utilization.

Utilizing Neuro-linguistic Programming to Increase Custom Clay Poker Chips Sales

On and when you are looking to expand the offers of your Custom Clay Poker Chips, you ought to consider actualizing the utilization of the neurolinguistic deals methodologies that many are utilizing - running from people who work an independent company to significant organizations. These systems depend on the way that our capacity to utilize language can help persuade others that the item and additional items that you offer are things that they need.

This business methodology is utilized to convince your intended interest group that the Clay Poker Chips that you offer are the best available, and are the ones that are indicated for them as people. Here, you will figure out how to utilize neurolinguistic Programming to build the offers of your Custom Clay Poker Chips!

Stage 1:

Before endeavoring to execute the utilization of neurolinguistics in deals, it is significant that you know and sees precisely what this is. It is a generally basic idea acquainted by what shows up with being a very inside and out word, or expression, contingent upon how it is composed or communicated. It is the investigation and research that encompasses how the psyche sees language.

It encompasses how the language is utilized, and how it is deciphered by those people that are acquainted with the words that are being verbally expressed. While this may appear to be a pointless way to advance the Custom Clay Poker Chips that you offer, it could demonstrate to be very productive at last. Despite what business that you take part in, neurolinguistic programming can be a powerful apparatus with regards to the benefits and by and massive accomplishment of your organization.

Stage 2:

When you have a fundamental comprehension of neurolinguistics, you should see some essential data about correspondence. Concerning your showcasing attempts, it is critical to speak to the faculties of the group of spectators that you need to target. You can excite the brain from various perspectives. If you have some expertise in Personalized Clay Poker Chips, you will need to hit on however many faculties as could reasonably be expected.

There is a piece of neurolinguistics that is alluded to as "word inventories." In this, it is accepted that one must portray a thing or numerous things in three different habits. The first is visual. This incorporates the "photos" that the brain really finds in your Professional Clay Poker Chips showcase attempt.

Stage 3:

When you have chipped away at the promoting procedure that enables your intended interest group to "see" what it is that you have, and "see" how the item, as well as items, can profit them and improve a mind-blowing nature, the time has come to proceed onward to the sound-related way. At last, you should relate a type of "sound" in your showcasing technique.

Thinking of you as are gaining practical experience in Pro Clay Poker Chips, it might be perfect for actualizing the sound of Poker Chips falling or hitting one another. When you have this, the time has come to proceed onward to the subsequent stage.

Stage 4:

Presently, your advertising technique to build your deals in Custom Clay Poker Chips has your intended interest group, really perceiving how they can profit by your item as well as items. It likewise has your intended interest group really "hearing" the hints of the game. It is presently time to get the sensation. This is regularly the most testing with regards to a promoting effort for an organization - paying little heed to what they sell.

This includes stimulating certain emotions in your potential clients, and in any event, upgrading faculties like that of touch. Will they "feel" the nature of the All Clay Poker Chips that they are being encouraged to buy? Do they partner positive sentiments from the idea of having a lot of Poker Chips that you are advertising? If not, the time has come to incorporate these viewpoints into your showcasing effort. It should all be possible with the utilization of language!

Stage 5:

Now, you might be asking, "what does this accomplish for deals?" That is the simple part! We are altogether extraordinary. We originate from various foundations, we as a whole have one of a kind encounters, and we as a whole procedure thing on an alternate level. While we utilize every one of the faculties that we can, we each have essential faculties, and auxiliary detects. We both learn and see outwardly, by sound, or by contact and feelings.

On and when you guarantee that your showcasing effort for the Custom Clay Poker Chips that you have incorporates each of the three indexes of visual segments, sound-related segments, and sensation parts you will speak to for all intents and purposes all characterizations of individuals who might be keen on owning Clay Poker Chips!

You need to pull in all strolls, a wide range of recognitions - all things considered, there are people in all classes that appreciate playing Poker! On and when you pursue these means on the most proficient method to utilize neurolinguistic programming to build the offers of your Custom Clay Poker Chips, you will, at last, find that you get more outcomes from your publicizing efforts!

CHAPTER THREE

MANAGING YOUR EMOTIONS

Dealing with your feelings is especially an issue of decision. Would you like to, or not? So much has been expounded on feelings and how to manage them adequately, yet numerous individuals can't control this everyday issue. Why? Overseeing feelings viably is really similar to building up ability or a propensity. It is a method for improving, and as people, we battle with change the most.

Changing how you generally accomplish something isn't simple, and it is much increasingly troublesome about feelings. At the point when we are feeling 'passionate,' the exact opposite thing we need to do is quiet down and attempt to manage the circumstance star effectively; we frequently need to yell about what is upsetting us.

On and when we comprehend somewhat more about how our feelings work, we are in a vastly improved situation to utilize this data to further our potential benefit. Figuring out how to control your feelings can be perhaps the best aptitude you will ever create in your life. Your feelings lead to the moves you make and in this way, make the existence you are encountering now, all aspects of it.

Our enthusiastic piece of the mind, the limbic framework, is perhaps the most established part when looked at, for instance, to our prefrontal cortex, which is our 'thinking' part. Since our enthusiastic part is so old, and in this way an incredibly solid piece of the mind, it is justifiable that it feels like our feelings run us and seize our intuition on occasion. The normal individual's enthusiastic piece of the cerebrum is more than six billion times more dynamic than the prefrontal cortex.

The fact is that your feelings will normally capture your reasoning—this is guaranteed—yet there are still approaches to manage this.

To keep things basic, how about we take a gander at what you can do to flip this circumstance around. Disregarding feelings, stifling them, or not managing them will return to haunt you! Stress and uneasiness originate from smothered feelings, so on, and when you believe that managing your feelings by disregarding them is getting down to business, you are woefully off-base.

As indicated by numerous neuro phonetic programming methods, there are three components to any expertise or conduct. These three components are interconnected, and when you change one, you consequently change the others.

To start with, there is the outside conduct, which is the thing that the individual really does or says. Furthermore, the individual's inside procedures or musings, and thirdly the individual's inward states or feelings. The following are two simple and basic approaches to deal with your feelings successfully. Utilize this basic technique to oversee disappointment, outrage, bitterness, dread, or some other negative feeling. These are fundamental neuro-semantic programming systems.

1. Change your physiology.

Changing your physiology is presumably the least complex neuro etymological programming system to change your feelings in a split second. You can prepare yourself to change your physiology to feel confident, excellent, rich, glad, settled, or grateful. To do that, become mindful of your physical body when you're miserable, baffled, or terrified of something. Is it accurate to say that you are drooped or slouched over? Any tight muscles in your shoulders, back, or legs? Are your eyebrows wrinkled, your eyes squinted, or perhaps your jaw gripped? At that point, change your physiology immediately, move, lift your hands over your head or bounce around as high as possible. As you do this, see how your feelings and thinking have changed.

2. Change your reasoning.

It's less of what you think yet how you think it. I took in a basic neuro phonetic programming procedure years prior called the cloud method. You can likewise consider the entryway strategy. Envision two entryways or two veils of mist before you, one to your left side and one to your right side. At the point when you experience a negative feeling, which is spoken to by a cloud, step away from it (the feeling and the cloud). Ask yourself the two after inquiries: does this feeling serve me in that circumstance? Ideally, your answer is no. At that point, asks yourself: what other helpful feelings I would require in that circumstance. At the point when you think that its, make as though it was the subsequent cloud or the subsequent entryway and start strolling to the entryway or bouncing in the cloud in your creative mind. You just ventured away from a negative feeling and submerged yourself into an increasingly clever state.

With training, you can ace your feelings. It can take you 10 minutes to do it the first run through, yet it will just take you seconds with training.

You can't generally control what befalls you, yet you can control your reaction. It isn't tied in with disregarding how you feel; rather, you have to comprehend your feelings and utilize this comprehension to pick your reaction to a troublesome circumstance. Doing this work will lessen the impact of weight on your wellbeing, improve your basic leadership, and backing everyone around you in accomplishing ideal outcomes.

Here are ten stages to take to deal with your feelings in those profoundly charged minutes.

1. Distinguish and name your feelings. Check-in with yourself a few times each day to see how you are feeling. On and when you wind up utilizing general words like fine, OK, or great to portray your feelings, drive yourself to be increasingly explicit and perceive the nuances of your feelings. On and when you can't locate the correct words, possibly you have to grow your passionate jargon. A web search on "arrangements of feelings" will yield arrangements of feelings that you can use as a source of perspective.

2. Recognize feelings and contemplations. Contemplations and feelings are inseparably connected. Much the same as the incredible chicken and egg banter that researchers have had

for a considerable length of time, it is hard to figure out what starts things out? Yet, our contemplations do make a passionate encounter. Your contemplations can make physical sensations as your body responds to what you state as though it were genuine. Construct consciousness of your "self-talk" and the physical sensations related to various feelings. This procedure of becoming more acquainted with yourself at an alternate level will fabricate your mindfulness and capacity to deal with your feelings.

3.   Skill to quiet yourself down and postpone your response. It might be as straightforward as taking long moderate breaths. The old procedure of tallying to ten really works as a method for quieting enthusiastic responses and giving time for viewpoint. In any event, concentrating on taking notes, or doodling an image for yourself, can be a gainful imaginative discharge. Keep in mind that you have control of your responses. You can't stop the breeze; however, you can give it a chance to spill off your sails! Before you respond to a circumstance, allow yourself to think and pull it together to abstain from saying something that you are probably going to lament.

4.   Acknowledge your feelings. Overseeing feelings isn't tied in with passing judgment on a feeling as either fortunate or

unfortunate and afterward covering the awful ones. Emotions don't leave since you overlook them. The dreamer technique of disregarding your emotions may give impermanent help, yet it's conceivable that the sentiments will return considerably more grounded than previously. A little dissatisfaction can prompt outrage or slight worry to freeze. Acknowledge your feelings as data about yourself.

5.   Turn the spotlight internal to reflect and get yourself. Consider the circumstances or individuals that annoyed you. Do you see any examples in your responses? Burrow further to comprehend your responses and hot catches. What are your programmed examples of thought? What suppositions would you say you are making as you make inferences from your perceptions? Are you over-summing up, mind perusing, accusing, or foreseeing what's to come? Gain from your reactions and the responses they trigger in others, deciding how you may react unexpectedly.

6.   Build up a propensity for positive self-talk. The running critique in your mind is with you day in and day out and can affect your recognitions and frame of mind. If your self-talk is negative, it will make your negative reality. Consider the objectives that you need to accomplish and afterward recognize progressively beneficial musings that help these

objectives. Whenever you get yourself in negative self-talk, stop and check whether you can re-outline your reasoning utilizing these progressively valuable considerations.

7. Exercise. An extraordinary method to consume off disappointment and stress is a workout. Any physical activity is a solid outlet for enthusiastic vitality, and it will enable your body to be increasingly impervious to push. Start gradually, however, have an ordinary program of physical activity with the goal that when the weight is on, you are stronger and ready to keep your cool.

8. Express your emotions appropriately. Feelings are the magic that binds connections. In the work environment, the passionate vitality of the pioneer can help characterize the way of life. Be that as it may, there is a major contrast between conveying everything that needs to be conveyed deferentially and "giving them a chance to have it." Talk and recognize how you feel; however, consistently know about the effect on others. Feelings can demolish a culture, or they can help make a working environment that is loaded with vitality, bounty, good faith, advancement, and trust - prompting achievement.

9. Now and again, you simply need to vent. Discharging our feelings can go about as a security valve - easing pressures,

much the same as steam out of a pot. On and when you truly need to vent, discover somebody you trust outside the circumstance that will simply hear you out. Perceive that although blustering may feel great at the time, it is a way to nowhere, except if you set aside the effort to reflect and comprehend your feelings. Additionally, fuming may simply fan the fire and exacerbate the situation.

10. Practice, practice, practice. The more you practice the means over, the more you will flex, manufacture, and deal with your enthusiastic muscle.

Dealing with your Emotion

You are better put into dealing with your feelings since you realize your issues best. You have to have the correct instruments that will direct you in realizing how to deal with the feelings correctly. Stress is a condition that influences all individuals from varying backgrounds along these lines, don't believe that there is some problem with you when you wind up focused. There are numerous things that reason pressure, and they are generally negative awful things. Remember or compose everything that might be causing your concern. It may be a loss of occupation, loss of a friend or family member, destitution, low self-suppositions because of different factors thus substantially more.

Keep in mind that there might be more than one stressor at work affecting you to be pushed.

When you have the stressors, you have to neutralize them and start to sustain yourself with inspiration. You may need to leave behind certain organizations, and a few people wind up, leaving a place of employment for their wellbeing. Remember that the arrangements of a specific issue having a place with someone else won't work for you. You have to encircle yourself with constructive individuals who have a sound point of view. Your feelings are a crucial piece of you and on, and when you free the heading of overseeing yourself, your life will likewise be influenced. Some things will help you manage your feelings viably, and they incorporate the accompanying.

You have to give your feelings a chance to direct you or at the end of the day, don't manage your feelings, what you feel. For instance, on and when you are in a distressing circumstance where you believe you have to cry, do not dither. Make sure that all your outside elements are working great, and they are appropriate, this incorporates the suppers that you take in which must be adjusted and sound.

Whenever left unchecked, sentiments can hold us hostage and keep us from encountering genuine joy. Sentiments are genuine, yet we should discover what it is we're truly feeling. We regularly need to make preparations for uncertain feelings from our past that contrarily influences our present circumstance. For instance, if a past relationship left you feeling uncertain and less, at that point certain about yourself, don't extend that feeling into your present relationship.

Outrage and unforgiveness are feelings that stunt us into accepting we're in an ideal situation without the culpable individual. If we harbor outrage, it will obliterate us, frequently prompting forlornness and physiological issues. Although we might be defended, it looks bad to enable resentment to control us. You will blow up; however, manage it immediately. Try not to allow it to putrefy, causing more harm and a bigger crack in your connections.

Delight, distress, agony, and love are significant notions. God gave us feelings with the goal that we could really react to extraordinary seasons. Feelings are a benchmark for the profound activities of our spirit and enable us to convey what needs to be. Feelings have a spot; simply don't give them a chance to manage your life.

Our feelings can serve to lift us to extraordinary statures or thwart our self-improvement. One of the systems which may become helpful in dealing with your feelings is to get careful or mindful of them as they happen. For some individuals, they stay snoozing with regards to the idea of their feelings; the job they serve in their life. Through the rehashed presentation of figuring out how to distinguish and deal with your feelings, you have a superior comprehension of how they may best serve you. It requires some investment, persistence, and steadiness.

Look at your feelings. What feelings are serving you at present? Is it accurate to say that they are helpful? To comprehend the feeling and perhaps reframe it, you have to look at the conviction behind it - for that is the fuel. On and when the feeling is one of bitterness, outrage, or nervousness, take a gander at whether it is serving your most noteworthy development. The Buddhist guideline states if the feeling isn't vital, "drop it - put it down" as if it were a knapsack. It's intended to be as basic as that, yet not exactly so practically speaking.

If you end up becoming violently unhinged when a friend or family member accomplishes an inappropriate thing by you, inspect the feeling. Address it - "what do you need me to know or learn outrage?" Look back to the conviction encompassing the feeling. I can guarantee you that your cherished one isn't the reason or the trigger of your feeling. It's the significance you joined to it when he/she neglected to ring you while they were voyaging interstate on business. You joined importance and doled out a feeling to it, which served a result - regardless of whether positive or negative.

At the point when you're living in an arrangement with your actual self, you build up a profound comprehension and association with self. You're in arrangement with your feelings, contemplations, and convictions. They start to serve you, as opposed to neutralizing you. You create inward harmony, concordance, satisfaction, and ecstasy. You transmit energy, excitement - everyone around you is attracted to you like a moth to a fire. Start now. Take responsibility forever. Put time and persistence in becoming more acquainted with you. You'll pull in the most stunning connections (business, individual, proficient, personal, kinship) and make a real existence deserving of thriving and bounty.

Four basic strides to begin controlling your feelings adequately.

1. The First Step Is Awareness

When you don't know about the occasions when you are excessively enthusiastic or going overboard, how might you attempt to oversee it? It is unimaginable. Begin to screen your feelings and offer names to them. Now and then, we think that it's hard to recognize what we are feeling. Giving it a name encourages us to gain lucidity, which is fundamental in pushing ahead.

2. Find the 'Why' of Your Emotions

When you have recognized how you are feeling, you need to find why you are feeling it. What is causing this inclination inside you? Obviously, there could be a million reasons, and to discover you need to ask yourself, similar to you would a companion, "What's going on? What is making me feel along these lines?" Your mind will consistently search for an answer.

More often than not, just how you are considering the circumstance is making you feel how you do. Another huge motivation behind why we feel negative feelings is because our qualities are absent at that time or being regarded.

Keep in mind: find the 'why.'

3. At that point, Ask Yourself, "What Is the Solution?"

When you have found why, what would you be able to do to reclaim control? Some of the time, you may need to change how you are pondering the circumstance.

Your contemplations lead legitimately to your sentiments, so if you are feeling terrible, you no doubt have a negative idea that is making you feel that way. On and when you start considering other potential methods for taking a gander at the circumstance, you will start to feel better right away. What you center around grows!

Now and again, by essentially understanding why you feel a specific route at a particular time, your feelings will begin to decrease since seeing consistently prompts quieting.

4. Pick How You Want to React

This is the hardest part. How we respond and deal with our feelings is a propensity. Haven't you seen those individuals who get worried about nothing, actually blowing a gasket at nothing? You nearly feel frustrated about them. They have made a propensity for partner a circumstance they don't care for with 'going ballistic.' Their feelings have seized them.

Figuring out how to tune in to your feelings, to distinguish, comprehend, and afterward pick them, isn't something that you choose to rehearse two times per week at noon. No, it is with constant exertion and control that you can begin to fabricate this basic aptitude.

9 Simple Tips to Help You Manage Your Emotions

As a therapist, given a ton of thought to how to have a more advantageous existence by dealing with your feelings. Here is a portion of my considerations, which I communicated in my book, "The Emotional Revolution."

Feelings can have a significant impact on physical wellbeing, and it is basic to manage the emotions that go with ordinary good and bad times of life.

9 Steps to Help Manage Your Emotions:

1. Utilize your feelings and strong reactions to perceive when you are under pressure. A hustling beat, dry mouth, hurting stomach, tight muscles, or muscle torment may all demonstrate that something is out of order in your passionate world.

2. Record your considerations and emotions about what is focusing on you. Take a day by day stock of your feelings. By recording what you feel and when you might have the option to recognize examples of passionate high points and low points. On and when is additionally imperative to record the musings that go with the emotions.

3. Control whatever part of the pressure that you can. Life presents numerous circumstances consistently, and you ought not to see them in high contrast terms-those you can

control versus those you can't. Search for the shades of dark the components you can control. At the point when you realize what will occur in a circumstance, your sensory system can equip to deal with it.

4.   Try not to make mountains out of molehills. At the point when troublesome circumstances emerge, it is essential to survey how terrible they truly are before going into alarm mode. On and when you need to carry on with a low-stress life, don't get all worked up over minor issues.

5.   Reclassify the Problem. Your demeanor to stress can influence your wellbeing beyond what the pressure itself can. If the issue is out of your control, perceive that and rethink the issue to figure out which parts you can maintain a strategic distance from or handle.

6.   Create practices that occupy you from stress. Anything you do that diverts you from your worry for some time is great. For instance, go for a stroll or work in the nursery.

7.   Connect with a companion or a relative. Social connections are useful for your wellbeing, and contacting somebody about your pressure can improve your standpoint. On and when you are deficient with regards to informal communities,

you may think that it's most straightforward to meet others during a mutual movement.

8.   Exercise Regularly. Standard practice is useful for your physical and enthusiastic wellbeing. Indeed, even moderate exercise can help decrease pressure.

9.   Ponder and Relax. Reflection has a wide assortment of medical advantages, and stress decrease is one of the enormous ones.

5 Tips in Managing Emotions

Avoid Triggers

You thought this enthusiastic thing was simple, correct? Award it for certain individuals; it is simple. Some individuals are commonly laid back and have an idea about this enthusiastic thing. Bravo, however, for all of us, we have to choose our fights. Focus on what triggers you. Is it somebody taking your parking spot or somebody who didn't state a "thank you" for a blessing? You are not supporting the conduct that you are simply going to maintain a strategic distance from circumstances or have a procedure to proceed onward. Pick another stopping place, have a reinforcement, or in the event of the discourteous blessing taker, center around the part of giving without getting something back as a "much obliged."

Avoid Jumping the Gun

Try not to respond immediately as this will put you on the way of conceivable obliteration. Settle on the choice to do nothing until you have chilled off. Leave for a minute and inhale profoundly for five minutes the Huffington Post shared. "Keep on breathing profoundly for five minutes, feeling like your muscles intense, and your pulse comes back to ordinary." Feel better? If not, devise an arrangement early on what should be possible to occupy you from the pressure. Go for a stroll, supplicate, have some espresso, or play music. Acknowledge that you can't control every one of the difficulties throughout everyday life, except you can control how you respond to them.

Be Optimistic

Be an idealistic individual and change your mentality. This will help with unpleasant circumstances and help to adapt to wild feelings. We realize the pressure is unsafe for our wellbeing. If we are increasingly idealistic about existence, we will live more advantageous lives. Start with positive self-talk. This not exclusively will support feelings, the body, however the psyche. It could help with wretchedness, lessen strain, and decrease the danger of cardiovascular sicknesses. Changing your reasoning presently will pay for itself later as the psyche and feelings are associated. Saddle musings and discharge them when they are dangerous. Attempt music, nature, or a side interest to have an outlet when life gets to you. By and large, by turning out to be progressively idealistic and positive we

Be Grateful

Be appreciative and think about the beneficial things throughout everyday life. This will help quiet you down and will direct your mind-set. Appreciation takes your brain off yourself and celebrates what you as of now have. It can likewise enable forlornness, to bring down hostility and help with melancholy. Have a go at excusing yourself after you fall away from overseeing feelings that you are just human. It will be a procedure. Advise yourself that easy-going others will likewise enable you to pick appreciation, as opposed to nourishing into negative feelings, particularly after you feel insulted. If this is still difficult to do, connect with a companion to keep you responsible, and to enable you to vent.

Letting Go

There are more significant things in life than cutoff times, work, satisfying individuals, and having feelings that standard you. See the master plan and that your feelings are short-lived. Stop the hyper center around circumstances that are bothering. We need not give it a chance to affect our hours after the fact. Release it. Releasing the feelings is startling as it is a demonstration of giving up, and we feel that we are aloof, yet this isn't valid. Dropping the offense can be seen as an activity - a change we as a whole can partake in. It's fine to cry or hit a pad out of dissatisfaction. We have to have an arrival of negative sentiments as it is solid.

CHAPTER FOUR

HOW TO USE NLP TO MANAGE EMOTIONS

n NLP, there is nothing of the sort as an un-creative individual, only an un-ingenious state. Having the option to deal with your state so you can stay creative even in the most testing circumstances is unmistakably something that is of gigantic worth any place you work, whatever you do and whoever you are!

Whatever task you need to play out, anything you desire the result to be, ask yourself - "what state would I like to be in to make this simple?"

On and when you would like to or need to change your state to assist you with performing at your ideal level, then there are numerous approaches to do so utilizing NLP procedures.

To kick you off, here are three simple approaches to assist you in dealing with your passionate state:

1. Core interest

Change the photos you are making for yourself – what you are envisioning, yet how you imagine it. Change the sounds you can hear, become progressively mindful, and zone in for the ideal picture. Ever seen what occurs if you're feeling low or somewhat askew and, at that point, you hear your preferred bit of inspiring music? Change the sounds and how you envision your final product to be.

2. Physiology

Change your body profoundly – Move, do whatever pushes various synthetic concoctions around your sensory system, whether this could be accomplishing more exercise or just taking the stairs rather than the lift. Change your stance, stand tall, high, and effective, not exclusively will you look certain, yet you'll feel increasingly sure. Consider changing your outward appearance as well, and your breathing, even the littlest revises, will assist you in dealing with your state.

3. Self-Talk

Change your inside exchange or self-talk. You can change the substance or the language of your mind jabber, so you become your very own hero. What about changing the inside pundit that discloses to you that you're bad enough? Envision how amusing you may discover it if your internal pundit had the voice of Mickey Mouse or the Donkey from Shrek? Or then again move the area of the voices, so it originates from your left huge toe!

All states are brought about by the association between your reasoning designs, your physiology, and your neurochemicals. Changing any of these can impact your state.

The capacity to change your state and pick how you feel is one of the abilities for the passionate opportunity and cheerful life. Passionate opportunity doesn't mean failing to feel negative, but that you are increasingly mindful of negative states and can pick your reaction.

There are numerous manners by which individuals can build up mindfulness to adequately deal with their states. This is only one of the numerous incredible procedures in NLP to assist you with performing at your best regardless of what is happening in your condition.

Improve enthusiastic insight with NLP

As we find out increasingly more about what makes individuals an accomplishment in business and particularly regarding administration, the widespread supposition is moving ceaselessly from the conventional traits of IQ and specialized capacity and towards enthusiastic insight. Passionate knowledge is currently observed as a "need to have" fixing in the makeup of pioneers.

In contrast to our IQ, our enthusiastic knowledge is something that can be created and improved with preparing, and NLP Training does only that. Passionate insight is portrayed in its Wikipedia passage as "the capacity to recognize, evaluate, and control the feelings of oneself, others, and gatherings."

Enthusiastic Intelligence

Five components of our make-up that we could ascribe to passionate knowledge at work:

Mindfulness – How much do we comprehend about our very own temperaments, states, and feelings and how they sway on our conduct? Is it accurate to say that we are mindful of how our states of mind influence others? How effectively would you say you are ready to distinguish your very own qualities and shortcomings, qualities, needs, and drives?

Self Regulation – How great would we say we are at intuition before we act? It is safe to say that we are ready to control our states of mind and motivations to maintain a strategic distance from our conduct, having negative ramifications for other people and us?

Inspiration – How solid is your longing to seek after your objectives perseveringly? How are your general vitality levels? Do you have an enthusiasm forever and for your work that is past cash and power?

Sympathy – How simple do we discover it to see someone else's perspective? What amount do we comprehend about the enthusiastic make-up of other individuals? How effectively do we adjust our very own conduct in the light of other individuals' passionate responses?

Social Skills – How effectively would you say you are ready to assemble affinity and discover shared opinions to deal with your connections adequately?

NLP tends to every last one of these zones, and NLP Training is intended to work at the oblivious level to ensure that just as recognizing what you ought to do, you can exhibit skill in really doing it. It is just through preparing conduct into your sensory system that the conduct gets changeless and repeatable, and this is cultivated by working with the intuitive piece of your cerebrum.

NLP improves enthusiastic knowledge

How about we take a gander at how explicitly NLP can profit you as far as the five components referenced previously:

Self Awareness

In the NLP Practitioner course, the underlying spotlight is on building up a comprehension of how your cerebrum works, how you develop your encounters, and how your conduct is created. This empowers you to comprehend and perceive your mind-sets and states and see how you have achieved those dispositions and states.

A lot of NLP Submodalities work is tied in with empowering you to change your musings, feelings, different preferences by comprehension, and controlling the better qualifications in the considerations that your procedure.

Self-Regulation

NLP Anchoring empowers you to perceive and change your temperament in a moment. It additionally empowers you to set up triggers that will naturally deliver a positive feeling in you under explicit conditions. This can be helpful for circumstances where you ordinarily find that you carry on ineffectively previously.

In the Strategies part of the NLP Practitioner course, we figure out how we have specific oblivious reasoning techniques that make up our practices. We figure out how to dismember these systems and change them to deliver better conduct in our quest for greatness.

Motivation

NLP is about results. It is tied in with choosing what you need, how you need to improve, and finding a course to prevail with regards to arriving.

Utilizing NLP Submodalities and Timeline procedures, you can make your objectives and targets convincing and direct your vitality towards accomplishing them.

Neurological Level is a piece of the NLP Practitioner preparing, and this reasoning empowers you to guarantee that you work, prepare and set targets for yourself as well as other people at a level that gives you reason and empowers you to accomplish any profound goals that you may have.

Empathy

Perceptual Positions is a fun practice that you learn in the NLP Practitioner course where you get to re-experience a past occasion where you have had correspondence trouble with somebody, and you survey the circumstance from three heavenly attendants. You see the circumstance from your very own position, the situation of the other individual, and from the situation of a fly on the divider. This truly empowers you to start to make superior compassion with others and to see things from alternate points of view.

In NLP, Sensory Acuity is tied in with perceiving minute changes in someone else that part with how they are thinking, empowering you to perceive their states of mind, their temperament changes, and their feelings.

The entire prospectus of NLP Master Practitioner preparing is equipped around empowering you to comprehend other individuals and what really matters to them. You figure out how to comprehend your own and different people group's esteem and characters along these lines empowering you to all the more likely adjust working undertakings to their inclinations and all the more likely propel them.

Social Skills

NLP gives a procedure to "getting in Rapport" with someone else. There are such a large number of ways that you can pick up compatibility with somebody, and a considerable lot of them are oblivious, so you don't have the foggiest idea of how you did it. In some cases, you have compatibility and feel that vivacious association with individuals and different occasions you don't. NLP Rapport process empowers you to comprehend what makes affinity intentionally and to make it, without fail deliberately!

NLP shows you how to assemble compatibility utilizing your breathing, the words that you use, the sentences that you build, how you hold your body. This empowers individuals to all the more likely impact others.

The advantages of creating enthusiastic insight utilizing NLP

There are immediate advantages in utilizing NLP to build up your enthusiastic insight, here is the thing that you will understanding:

- Mindfulness – Improved fearlessness, genuineness.
- Self-Regulation – Increased honesty and receptiveness to change.
- Inspiration – Optimism, solid drive to succeed and accomplish, improved duty.
- Sympathy – Improved capacity to work with others, construct incredible groups, and hold the best individuals. Heavenly relational abilities.

- Social Skills –the increased capacity to impact and convince others and lead change.

What is NLP? These four methods could change how you think

Neuro-etymological programming (NLP) is frequently used to improve relational elements. It additionally has applications in self-awareness and improvement. A few NLP procedures can assist you with living a progressively glamorous and important life.

NLP underscores the significance of acing higher mindfulness strategies to spot examples, considerations, and suspicions that can be keeping you from discovering the joy in your life. Here are four important NLP methods that you can utilize and the science behind them.

1. Mooring

Mooring is one of the most well-known NLP strategies. The objective is to inspire positive reactions freely by partner a specific mental and passionate state to a grapple, which can be a picture, a word, or a motion. Tying down improves our capacity to control feelings and to play a functioning job in self-administration, making us less inclined to feeling feeble and overpowered.

Step by step instructions to utilize the mooring procedure

- Elicit when you encountered the extreme positive inclination you need to trigger in different circumstances (for example, feeling accomplishment the minute you got an advancement).
- Bring in tactile prompts related to that state (for example, what you saw, felt, smelt, heard).
- Bring the memory to its most extreme point and afterward partner your emotions to a stay (for example, bend a ring on your finger, squeeze your ear cartilage).
- Take a brief break and rehash the means above.
- Test the stay (for example, squeeze your ear cartilage) to inspire the extraordinary sentiment of accomplishment.
- You would then be able to utilize this strategy at whatever point you need an enthusiastic lift me-up, either all alone or close by other NLP procedures.

Securing depends on the mental idea of molding, whereby an upgrade triggers certain reactions. Tying down causes you evoke the reaction you need through redundancy. It benefits you by placing you accountable for your feelings. Also, a few investigations propose that when combined with different methods and intercessions, securing can help defeat fears and silly feelings of trepidation.

2. Reframing

Next in the rundown of NLP methods is 'reframing' or review unfriendly occasions from an alternate 'outline.' This enables you to open up your psyche to circumstances that might be lying ahead as opposed to harping on the negatives. To put it plainly, reframing changes the concentration from negative and overwhelming to positive and enabled.

The most effective method to reframe an idea, feeling, or conduct:

- Identify the idea, feeling or conduct you need to change.
- Establish contact with the deepest piece of yourself that is setting off the negative state of mind. This could be a picture, voice, articulation, and so on.
- Find the positive aim behind that part. Suppose you have a dread of flying. The sound of a plane's motor taking off triggers tension since it needs to secure you. This goal is great; however, the reaction is lacking.

- Focusing on the positive goal, attempt a few different ways of reacting that will assist you with acknowledging such aim. For instance, recognize the assurance and self-protection, which is the reason you pick the most secure method for voyaging (flying versus driving).

- Ensure your intuitive is completely dedicated to attempting elective reactions, and that it won't disrupt your reframing endeavors. Check for clashing convictions, and on and when you wind up rationalizing, return to stage four and discover elective methods for reacting.

Reframing is utilized as a restorative method for its capacity to change discernments. Various parts of the cerebrum trigger recollections and feelings: recollections are put away in the hippocampus, while the amygdala primarily controls feelings.

While reviewing past occasions, the amygdala reacts by setting off a feeling that duplicates the first one; however, reframing helps us that the nature to remember that feeling isn't fixed and that we can break programmed designs and organize sound reactions over automatic responses. Reframing is one of those NLP systems that demonstrate it's conceivable to break free from the purported amygdala capture.

3. Meta-demonstrating

Meta-demonstrating is one of the most dominant NLP systems, given its capacity to help distinguish willful limitations that might be keeping you from discovering bliss. The most straightforward approach to meta-model is by taking a gander at the language you use in regular daily existence, focusing on these three sorts of examples:

- Generalizations, prove in considerations along the lines of "I'm generally so unfortunate" or "all men are the equivalent."
- Distortions: mind perusing (for example, "John didn't welcome me today, he should be annoyed with me") or cause-impact articulations (for example, "if I don't get in shape, I will feel like a disappointment").
- Deletions, or carefully selecting your comprehension of reality to affirm previous convictions. For example, somebody with poor confidence would disregard compliments and give undue consideration to scrutinizes, prompting contemplations like "individuals don't discover me appealing."

Instructions to utilize meta demonstrating:

Recognize which class your considerations have a place with; at that point, start the exploratory procedure of scrutinizing the maladaptive idea design. For instance, if you get yourself in an erasure like "individuals don't discover me appealing," meta-demonstrating inquiries to pose would be "which individuals explicitly?" and "how would you realize that?".

The odds are that your answers will incorporate a summed up proclamation with the words "consistently" or "never," at that point, it's a great opportunity to ask yourself whether you are reasonable by asserting that things are consistently along these lines and never that way. When meta-displaying, it's additionally helpful to get some information about elective approaches. For instance, in the announcement, "if I don't get more fit, I'll feel like a disappointment," ask yourself in the case of feeling like a disappointment is your lone choice.

Meta-displaying works since it compels you to challenge imbued reaction designs that can develop into what specialists in mental science call over the top shirking conduct, which confines your capacity to gain from new encounters. The adequacy of this procedure is likewise connected to the design division. At the point when looked with another circumstance, we will in general contrast and past ones, yet on and when example division is dynamic, you will comprehend that various situations require various reactions.

4. The Swish Method

This is one of the NLP methods that accentuate the seriously constraining impact of negative contemplations. The objective of the Swish strategy is to distinguish mental and passionate triggers of pessimism and supplant them with a perfect reaction. When utilizing the Swish procedure, you don't need to make any move, however, become mindful of the options accessible and train your cerebrum to set off a "more joyful mode" at whatever point negative contemplations and feelings start to overwhelm you.

Step by step instructions to place the Swish Method enthusiastically:

- Identify the inclination that triggers nervousness. Model: you might be on edge about test execution even though you have given a valiant effort to get ready for it. For this situation, the trigger inclination would be anxiety and uneasiness.

- Next, know how your mind and body respond to such emotions (for example, nail gnawing, hitches in the stomach, and so on.) Create a visual picture of the setting wherein this occurs (for example, as you stroll into the test room).

- Think about how you might in a perfect world want to react as you physically enter the setting wherein the negative contemplations happen (for example certain, decidedly ready, idealistic, and so on.).

- This is known as the substitution suspected. In your psyche, envision the negative state and allegorically place the substitution thoroughly considered it, ensure it seems greater, more grounded, and increasingly energetic while causing the negative feeling to show up in highly contrasting or hazy.

As it occurs with other NLP systems for joy, you have to rehearse the Swish Method a couple of times to guarantee the substitution thought turns into the default reaction. Do it, at any rate, multiple times and accelerate the representation with each round. To check for viability, summon the trigger idea or feeling and its specific circumstance, and perceive how you feel about it.

The Swish Method is a representation procedure driven by the rule that truth can be stranger than fiction. The research examines demonstrated that the mind doesn't separate among genuine and imagined occasions, as the two of them actuate similar pieces of the cerebrum. Different examines have indicated that the sort of mental practice associated with representation directly affects essential subjective aptitudes, including memory, consideration, and discernment. The advantages of acing this system incorporate improved enthusiastic execution and a quiet and certain methodology, realizing that you don't have to give negative musings a chance to rule your life.

CHAPTER FIVE

USING DARK PSYCHOLOGY TO MANAGE EMOTIONS

Negative Emotions and How to Control Them

What are the Negative Emotions?

It's essential to recognize what a feeling is and what an inclination is. While the two are interconnected, there's a greater distinction than you may understand. It's unquestionably something that shocked me when I started with my examination.

Feelings – Emotions are viewed as 'lower level' reactions. They initially happen in the subcortical regions of the mind, for example, the amygdala and the ventromedial prefrontal cortices. These territories are answerable for delivering biochemical responses that directly affect your physical state.

Feelings are coded into our DNA and are thought to have created as an approach to assist us with reacting rapidly to various ecological dangers, much like our 'battle or flight' reaction. The amygdala has additionally been appeared to assume a job in the arrival of synapses that are basic for memory, which is the reason enthusiastic recollections are frequently more grounded and simpler to review.

Feelings have a more grounded physical establishing than sentiments meaning specialists discover them simpler to gauge equitably through physical prompts, for example, bloodstream, pulse, mind movement, outward appearances, and non-verbal communication.

Sentiments – Emotions are viewed as going before emotions, which will, in general, be our responses to the various feelings we experience. Where feelings can have an increasingly summed up understanding over all people, sentiments are progressively emotional and are impacted by our encounters and elucidations of our reality dependent on those encounters.

Sentiments happen in the neocortical districts of the cerebrum and are the following stage; by the way, we react to our feelings as a person. Since they are so abstract, they can't be estimated how feelings can.

Clinicians have since quite a while ago investigated the scope of human feelings and their definitions. Eckman (1999) recognized six beginning essential feelings:

- Anger
- Disgust
- Fear
- Happiness
- Sadness
- Surprise

Later developed this to incorporate a further eleven fundamental feelings:

- Amusement
- Contempt
- Contentment
- Embarrassment
- Excitement
- Guilt
- Pride

- Relief
- Satisfaction
- Sensory Pleasure
- Shame

Contrary feelings "as a terrible or despondent feeling which is evoked in people to express an antagonistic impact towards an occasion or individual." Reading through the rundown of Eckman's essential feelings, it's straightforward to decide those that may be alluded to as 'adverse' feelings.

While we can utilize the name negative, with what we think about feelings, recognize that all feelings are totally typical to encounter. They are a piece of our instilled DNA. What is increasingly significant, is getting when and why negative feelings may emerge, and creating positive practices to address them.

A Look at the Psychology of Emotions

One of the more famous mental speculations of feelings is Robert Plutchik's Wheel of Emotions. Plutchik (1980) expressed that there are eight essential feelings: bliss, trust, dread, shock, misery, expectation, outrage, and appalling. Plutchik went further by blending the feelings with their contrary energies and afterward making the wheel of feelings, which serves to expound on how intricate and intuitive our feelings are.

Plutchik's wheel is a solid visual portrayal of how our feelings present themselves. As should be obvious, the center feeling diminishes as you move outward on the wheel. Plutchik likewise utilized shading to speak to the power of the feeling: the darker the shading, the more extraordinary it is. So at its most extraordinary trust becomes deference, and at any rate exceptional, acknowledgment.

It's a fabulous beginning asset for helping us further build up our comprehension of how our feelings present themselves, how they vacillate, and how they can cooperate. It has educated further mental research around there and is regularly the establishment from which specialists investigating feelings have based their examination.

A 'tree' of feelings which broke feelings into essential, optional, and tertiary measurements. This incorporates six essential feelings (love, euphoria, shock, outrage, pity, and dread), with related feelings that create at the auxiliary level, and again at the tertiary level. For instance, if the essential feeling is happiness, the auxiliary feelings could incorporate gladness, positive thinking or enthrallment, and the tertiary level could incorporate delight, triumph, what or expectation.

Another level and built up 'The Hourglass of Emotions.' In their book, they based on Plutchik's eight essential feelings and separated them into four measurements: affectability, consideration, loveliness, and fitness. They likewise made qualifications between which of the feelings were sure (satisfaction, trust, outrage, and expectation) or negative (nauseate, pity, dread, and shock).

8 Examples of Negative Emotions

As we've investigated, negative feelings are totally typical. Without them, we wouldn't have the option to acknowledge positive ones. Simultaneously, on and when you discover you reliably incline one specific feeling – particularly a negative one – it merits investigating why that may be.

8 of the more typical negative feelings and why they may emerge:

 # Anger

Ever have somebody let you know no to accomplish something you need? How does that make you feel? Does your blood start to heat up, your temperature rise, and do you figuratively 'see red'? This is regularly how outrage is portrayed. Your body is responding to things not going your direction, and it's an endeavor to attempt to amend that.

Regularly, when we're irate, we'll yell, our face will enlist our resentment, and we may even toss things around. We're attempting to get our specific manner in a circumstance, and this is the main way we can think how. In case you're frequently responding to situations along these lines, it's a smart thought to investigate why and think of progressively positive methodologies.

Annoyance

Do you have a partner who maybe talks too noisily? Does your accomplice consistently leave their filthy dishes in the sink? Although we may like our associate and love our accomplice, these practices can make us feel truly irritated. Alluding to Pluchik's wheel, you can see that inconvenience is the more fragile type of outrage. While not as extraordinary as an outrage, it's the aftereffect of a comparable perspective – something has occurred, or somebody is accomplishing something you wish they wouldn't. What's more, you do not influence it.

Fear

Dread is frequently referred to as one of the center's fundamental feelings, and that is because it's intensely connected with our feeling of self-protection. It's a developed reaction to caution us about hazardous circumstances, sudden deterrents, or disappointments. We don't feel dread to feel troubled, despite what might be expected, it's there to assist us with exploring potential risk effectively. Grasping the feeling of dread and investigating why it emerges can assist you in setting yourself up proactively to handle difficulties.

Anxiety

Much like dread, tension looks to caution us about potential dangers and threats. It's frequently observed as a negative feeling as it's idea having an on edge demeanor impedes judgment and our capacity to act. New look into has discovered the inverse.

Having tension elevated members' capacity to perceive faces with furious or dreadful demeanors. They estimated an electrical flag in the cerebrum and found that non-clinically analyzed members moved their vitality from tactile (communicating the feeling) to engine (physical activity) circuits. Essentially, members with uneasiness were progressively prepared to react and respond to apparent dangers.

Sadness

At the point when you miss a cutoff time, get an awful evaluation, or don't verify that activity you had your expectations stuck on, you'll likely feel pitiful. Misery happens when we are disappointed with ourselves, our accomplishments, or the conduct of another person around us. Bitterness can be great to encounter as it shows to us that we energetic about something. It very well may be an incredible impetus to seek after the change.

Guilt

Blame is a mind-boggling feeling. We can feel this in connection to ourselves and past practices that we wish hadn't occurred, yet also in connection to how our conduct impacts people around us. Blame is regularly alluded to as an 'ethical feeling' and can be another solid impetus to urge us to make changes throughout our life.

Apathy

Like blame, aloofness can be a perplexing feeling. If you've lost energy, inspiration, or enthusiasm for the things you've recently appreciated, this could be identified with a lack of care. Like outrage, it can emerge when we lose power over a situation or circumstance, yet as opposed to losing control, and we seek after a progressively aloof forceful articulation of insubordination.

Despair

Ever attempted to accomplish a specific undertaking or objective on numerous occasions and not succeeded? Did that make you want to toss your hands noticeable all around, and outdoors in bed with an enormous tub of frozen yogurt for an organization? That is sadness, and it's a feeling that emerges when we aren't getting the outcomes we need. Despondency gives us a reason to abandon our ideal objectives, and it returns to a self-safeguarding strategy. Gloom can really be a valuable suggestion to take a break and reestablish, before proceeding to seek after a difficult objective.

What Causes Negative Emotions and Why Do We Have Them?

When you start investigating negative feelings somewhat more, you can truly begin to perceive what may cause or trigger them, and why we have them in any case.

As far as causes, it could be various things, for instance:

- Anxiety looked about going to a meeting for a new position.

- Anger at being up to speed in rush hour gridlock.

- Sadness at encountering a separation.

- Annoyance that a partner hasn't taken the necessary steps for a major venture.

- Despair at not having the option to adhere to another exercise system.

Feelings are a wellspring of data that helps you comprehend what is happening around you. Negative feelings, specifically, can assist you with perceiving dangers and feel arranged to decidedly deal with potential threats.

Various encounters in our lives will induce distinctive passionate responses, to varying degrees of power. As a person, you will encounter a full scope of feelings all through your life in light of quickly evolving circumstances.

Would We Like to Overcome and Stop Negative Emotions Altogether?

It's typical for us to need to move away from feelings that make us feel awful. As a transformative reaction, negative feelings in the cutting edge world are not so much a sign of danger against us; however, surviving and halting them by and large would be tremendously unfavorable to us.

Negative feelings are an extraordinarily typical, sound, and accommodating piece of life. I believe it's extremely significant not to fall into the 'bliss trap' of accepting that these feelings are an indication of shortcoming or low passionate knowledge. I know from individual experience that attempting to conceal away from negative feelings, can prompt further passionate torment.

As a person, you will encounter a full scope of feelings all through your life in light of quickly evolving circumstances. No feeling is without reason. It's the point at which we start to additionally investigate and comprehend the reason behind every feeling, that we adapt better approaches to react, which underpins our enthusiastic development and feeling of prosperity.

When investigating negative feelings, it's likewise essential to realize that they are by all accounts, not the only wellspring of data you approach. Before you follow up on any feeling, you ought to likewise look to investigate your past encounters, put away information and recollections, individual qualities, and wanted results for some random situation. Keep in mind – feelings are a low-level response, so you get the chance to choose how you react to them and not let them enslave your conduct.

What are the Effects of Negative Emotions?

While understanding that negative feelings are a solid piece of life is significant, there is a drawback to giving them an excess of a free rule.

On and when you invest a lot of energy harping on negative feelings and the circumstances that may have caused them, you could go into a winding of rumination. Rumination is the propensity to continue thinking, replaying, or fixating on negative passionate circumstances and encounters. In this winding of negative reasoning, you can wind up feeling more regrettable and more awful about the circumstance and yourself, the consequence of which could be various inconvenient impacts on your psychological and physical prosperity.

The issue with rumination is that it builds your cerebrum's pressure reaction circuit, which means your body gets pointlessly overwhelmed with the pressure hormone cortisol. There's extensive proof this is a driver for clinical sorrow.

Further research has connected the propensity to ruminate to various hurtful adapting practices, for example, indulging, smoking and liquor utilization, nearby physical wellbeing results, including a sleeping disorder, hypertension, cardiovascular malady, and clinical nervousness and despondency.

Another study found that individuals who enjoyed delayed rumination after an enthusiastic negative encounter took more time to recuperate from the physiological effect of the experience.

Rumination can be a troublesome escape clause to escape, particularly as the vast majority don't understand they're stuck in ruminating trench and rather accept they are effectively critical thinking. This can prompt further ramifications for mental and physical prosperity.

5 Proven Benefits of Negative Emotions

It's not all fate and anguish. At the point when dealt with well, negative feelings can have demonstrated advantages for our prosperity, and undeniably more research has been filled investigating this part of negative feelings.

1. Misery can assist you in giving more consideration to detail

Where positive feelings signal that everything is great in our prompt condition, negative feelings alert us that there are difficulties or new improvements that require our increasingly engaged consideration. Bitterness sends us the ready that something isn't right and asks us to direct our concentration toward for what reason this might be, what may be causing it, and what we have to do to fix it.

2. Outrage can be a solid spark to look for intercession

Outrage is just trailed by animosity in around 10% of situations. Outrage has been demonstrated to urge you to search out dynamic practices to address situations or individuals you've discovered hazardous however doesn't really mean through showdown or physical acts. Outrage is a solid ready that urges you to consider why somebody may be carrying on a specific way, and what you can do to reestablish harmony.

3. Tension energizes better approaches for moving toward issues and difficulties

At the point when we feel on edge, we'll attempt to do anything we can not to feel that way any longer. Nervousness is firmly connected to our 'battle or flight' reaction, which enables your body to make vitality rapidly, good to go. At the point, when looked at risky circumstances, uneasiness will dominate and urge us to look for arrangements rapidly to escape peril.

4. Blame causes you to change negative conduct

Blame can be a particularly valuable feeling. It's basically our ethical compass, and when it goes off, it's a decent sign that we may have carried on or said something frightful to somebody we care about. It resembles our inside framework for rebuffing ourselves when we've accomplished something incorrectly. Individuals who are increasingly inclined to feeling remorseful are more averse to take, take drugs, resort to viciousness or drink and drive.

5. Desire persuades you to work more earnestly

Desire isn't constantly vindictive. More often than not, it's what analysts allude to as 'amiable envy.' Generous envy has been appeared to urge understudies to perform better on tests and in homework, as observing another understudy accomplish a decent evaluation made it increasingly substantial for them to accomplish as well. Next time you feel envious because another person has accomplished an ideal objective, attempt to consider this to be something worth being thankful for – it implies the objective is absolutely feasible for you as well.

How Might We Best Control and Deal with our Negative Emotions?

Probably the ideal approach to manage our negative feelings is through acknowledgment. Similarly, as there are advantages to negative feelings, driving ourselves to be cheerful all the time can likewise be averse to our general passionate prosperity.

Tolerating negative feelings, in ourselves as well as other people are, each of the pieces of being human enables us to manufacture better empathy for how they may introduce themselves and why. As opposed to getting stuck in an outlook that negative feelings should be kept away from or what they are in one way or another 'wrong' to encounter, we have to acknowledge they are a characteristic piece of what our identity is.

When we do that, we can truly start to change how we may react to them and create practices that are important and carry an incentive to how we convey what needs be and draw in with others.

6 Tips to Manage, Process and Embrace Negative Emotions

As positive brain science has increased more understanding of our negative feelings, it additionally had the option to furnish us with various methodologies for adjusting these feelings inside our everyday lives.

Approaches to proactively process and recognize negative feelings and thought of the abbreviation tears of would like to help mentor and guide people. This is what it represents:

T = Teach and Learn

This is the way toward tuning in to what your body is attempting to show you through the introduction of negative feelings and realize what they mean. It structures your very own insight into how you react to enthusiastic states, translating the sign your body is sending you, and recognizing that they fill a need.

E = Express and empower

Negative feelings urge us to express them. They are truly significant feelings. The express and empower some portion of the abbreviation urges you to investigate this with transparency and interest. It's tied in with expanding your acknowledgment of your normal senses and empowering them to be available without hatred.

A= Accept and get to know

This pursues on pleasantly from express and empower. It's tied in with getting to know yourself and how you are as a human. Concentrate on expanding your acknowledgment with positive certifications to bring your circle of negative feelings into a space of acknowledgment.

R = Re-assess and re-outline

When you've started to acknowledge this is a characteristic piece of what your identity is, you can start to concentrate on reframing the circumstance and how you respond. Because a negative feeling has emerged, it doesn't mean you need to respond in manners that are hindering you and the people around you.

Tolerating negative feelings isn't tied in with tolerating or pardoning poor practices; it's tied in with making mindfulness for oneself as well as other people to make constructive responses.

S = Social help

Realizing that negative feelings are available within each one of us, and in essentially a similar way, can be a phenomenal wellspring of sympathy and compassion to people around us. It's how we process our feelings that contrast, so observing somebody in the tosses of outrage, realizing that they are simply taking care of an apparent risk can truly urge us to move toward them with sympathy, instead of outrage ourselves.

H = Hedonic prosperity and joy

This is the way toward gathering positive encounters with negative. Since we all the more promptly review negative encounters, it very well may be helpful for us to gather them with positive encounters, so we don't fall into a ruminating trap. Along these lines, we can concentrate a greater amount of our vitality on reviewing the positive encounters.

O = Observe and visit

Set aside the effort to truly watch your responses without disregarding them, quelling them, or overstating them. Use care to carry your concentration to your mind and body and what a specific feeling is making inside you. Take care of these responses without judgment.

P = Physiology and conduct changes

Similarly, as you watch your enthusiastic and mental reactions, watch your physiological responses as well. Carry your concentration to your breath, your pulse, and sense out the adjustments in your physiology that a negative feeling may have caused. Once more, take care of these progressions without judgment.

E = Eudaimonia

This probably won't be a word you know about, yet it's well worth adding to your jargon. Eudaimonia is a Greek word that fundamentally alludes to having a decent soul. It implies you have discovered a condition of being that is cheerful, sound, and prosperous, and you have figured out how to take part in activities that outcome in your general prosperity. It implies you're effectively endeavoring towards a feeling of realness in everything you do.

Beneath tips to enable you to oversee, process, and grasp negative feelings in manners that will assist you with understanding and discover an incentive in them:

 # Envisage your 'Most ideal Self.'

If you have a feeling that your negative feelings are defeating you, that you're not communicating them in solid manners or stalling out in ruminating practices, a straightforward perception strategy could help.

Rather than concentrating just on the negative feeling or what you're fouling up, center rather around what you might want the conduct to be.

What does the ideal adaptation of you look like in that situation? How might they respond? What might they say? How might they feel? What might they do after? You can do this as a visual psychological exercise or a diary work out.

Taking the time once per week to rehearse, this can have astounding results on your state of mind as well as how you approach the situation next opportunity it comes around.

Practice Gratitude

Rehearsing appreciation has been appeared to have superb impacts for both the beneficiaries and providers. These impacts have long arrived at impacts on our temperament and impression of occasions, so it merits investing a smidgen of energy, adding the training to your week after week collection.

Regardless of whether it's for a little thing or a major thing, face to face, via telephone, a letter or a straightforward instant message, telling somebody you value them or something they have done, can truly have any effect by the way you see and react to negative feelings.

Explore care systems

On and when you discover you have a short breaker and outrage is your go-to negative feeling (or on and when you find you're generally on the range of the displeasure feeling, routinely encountering irritation) care could help to reframe what you're feeling.

Pursue the tears of expectation direction and set aside the effort to comprehend why you might be reacting along these lines. Care can assist you in finding the headspace to do this positively.

Learn how to react versus respond

Do you know the distinction between how you react versus how you respond? Negative feelings frequently urge us to respond promptly to a given situation. At the point when we feel furious, we may lash out or yell. At the point when we become miserable, we may pull back and dismiss individuals around us.

Now and again, we have to follow up on these driving forces, yet for the most part, we don't. By investigating your negative feelings, you can begin to build up your comprehension of how you respond and, instead, begin to change this to positive methods for reacting – which could mean discovering that any stretch requires no response of the imagination.

Know when to take a break

Realize when to take a day to yourself. If you are always encountering negative feelings and attempting to oversee them, your body is revealing to you something isn't right.

Take a day to re-focus. Fill this day with positive encounters, accomplishing the things that you know fuel you and make you feel better. This sort of break can realign your reasoning, give you some space to refocus on why you may be encountering the negative feelings, and think of some positive adapting systems.

8 Tips to Change Negative Thinking

Negative thinking adds to the tension in social and execution circumstances. Most treatments for social uneasiness include an angle devoted to changing negative speculation styles into progressively accommodating and positive methods for taking a gander at circumstances.

The way to changing your negative musings is to see how you think now (and the issues that outcome) and afterward, use systems to change considerations or make them have less impact. For the most part, these means are completed with an advisor; however, they can likewise be utilized as a component of a self-improvement exertion toward defeating social tension. The following are eight articles to assist you in changing your negative idea designs.

Understand Your Thinking Styles

One of the initial moves toward changing your negative reasoning examples is seeing precisely how you think at present. Here is a rundown of 10 kinds of "flawed" thinking designs that may be pushing you into difficulty.

For instance, on and when you will, in general, view yourself as a total achievement or disappointment in each circumstance, at that point, you are taking part in "highly contrasting" thinking. These ten reasoning examples vary in unobtrusive manners, yet they all include bends of the real world and nonsensical methods for taking a gander at circumstances and individuals.

How to Stop Thinking Negatively

One of the fundamental parts of a treatment plan, including intellectual conduct treatment (CBT), is subjective rebuilding. This procedure encourages you to distinguish and change your negative musings into increasingly supportive and versatile reactions.

Regardless of whether done in treatment or all alone, subjective rebuilding includes a bit by bit process whereby negative contemplations are distinguished, assessed for exactness, and afterward supplanted.

Although from the outset, it is hard to think with this new style, after some time and with training, positive and balanced considerations will come all the more regularly.

How to Cope With Criticism

Notwithstanding intellectual rebuilding, another part of CBT that is now and then supportive includes something known as the "confident guard of oneself." Since it is conceivable that a portion of the time, individuals will really be basic and critical, it is significant that you can adapt to dismissal.

This procedure is typically directed in treatment with an imagine discussion among you and your advisor to develop your confidence abilities and self-assured reactions to analysis. These abilities are then moved to this present reality through schoolwork assignments.

How to Practice Mindfulness

Care has its underlying foundations in reflection. It is simply the act of segregating from your contemplations and feelings and review them as an outside spectator.

During care preparing, you will figure out how to see your musings and emotions as articles gliding past you that you can stop and watch or let cruise you by.

The goal of care is to deal with your enthusiastic responses to circumstances by permitting the thinking part about your cerebrum to dominate.

Why Thought Stopping Doesn't Work

Thought halting is something contrary to care. It is the demonstration of being vigilant for negative musings and demanding that they are disposed of.

The issue with thought halting is that the more you attempt to stop your negative contemplations, the more they will surface. Care is desirable over idea halting because it gives less weight to your musings and diminishes the effect they have on you.

Figured halting may appear to help temporarily, yet in the long haul, it prompts more tension.

Understanding Thought Diaries

Thought journals are instruments that can be utilized as a feature of any procedure to change negative reasoning. Thought journals help you to recognize your negative reasoning styles and add a superior comprehension of how your contemplations (and not the circumstances you are in) cause your enthusiastic responses.

Most intellectual conduct treatment plans will include the utilization of an idea journal that you will finish as a feature of day by day schoolwork assignments.

Sample Thought Diary

Not sure what a real idea journal resembles? Here is an example structure that you can use to record your considerations and inspect the association between your negative reasoning styles and your enthusiastic responses.

How to Complete a Thought Diary

Here is a bit by bit portrayal of how to round out an idea journal like the example structure above.

In this specific model, we separate the perspective of an individual on the town and the enthusiastic and physical responses that outcome from negative reasoning examples.

Before the finish of the idea investigation, we have supplanted silly musings about dismissal with progressively supportive and positive perspectives.

CHAPTER SIX

USING PSYCHOLOGICAL WARFARE AND COGNITIVE BEHAVIORAL THERAPY (CBT) TO MANAGE EMOTIONS

Subjective social treatment (ordinarily alluded to as CBT) appears to consistently be in the news, with for all intents and purposes each new examination on brain science concentrated on CBT and its adequacy at treating an alternate mental issue. CBT is broadly perceived as the most bleeding edge, investigate upheld treatment for mental issues and disarranges. It speaks to the peak of current logical information on how the brain and feelings work. Various psychological conduct treatment practices have been created and tried by specialists everywhere throughout the world to locate the more viable, enduring answers forever's thorniest issues. Everything from tension and gloom to ADHD and socials abilities shortfalls has been the subject of CBT mediation and research. With each new investigation that is distributed, subjective social treatment practices are approved as the best quality of care in psychotherapy today.

What is Cognitive Behavioral Therapy (CBT)?

CBT gives a basic method for understanding moving circumstances and risky responses to them. Intellectual conduct treatment underscores three primary parts ensnared in mental issues: musings, feelings, and practices. By separating troublesome sentiments into these segment parts, it turns out to be extremely clear where and how to intercede when an issue emerges. On and when a specific negative idea is by all accounts, causing a chain response of negative feelings and conduct, the best arrangement might be to rethink that idea. On and when a standard of conduct appears to be mindful, another social reaction to the circumstance would probably be useful.

Frequently, every one of the three parts is intertwined, all through troublesome issues and emotions. Subjective social treatment practices are intended to meditate on every one of the three parts all the while. For example, when wild stress is the issue, CBT activities can help individuals to recognize increasingly powerful and grounded considerations, which diminishes tension. Thus, decreased tension makes it simpler to take part in handy conduct to effectively address the activating dangerous circumstance.

Cognitive Restructuring

Psychological rebuilding is a subjective conduct treatment practice intended to assist individuals with analyzing unhelpful reasoning examples and devise better approaches for responding to dangerous circumstances. Psychological rebuilding frequently includes keeping an idea record, which is a method for following useless programmed contemplations and conceiving versatile elective reactions.

Activity Scheduling

Movement booking is a psychological conduct treatment practice that assists individuals with taking part in practices they conventionally would maintain a strategic distance from, because of despondency, uneasiness, or different impediments. The mediation includes distinguishing compensating low-recurrence conduct and discovering time during the time to plan the conduct to build its recurrence. It is frequently utilized in treatment for wretchedness, as a method for re-bringing remunerating practices into individuals' schedules. While apparently basic, it is a central part of Behavioral

Activation, the best observationally upheld treatment for clinical misery.

Psychological Behavioral Therapy Exercises: Activity Scheduling

Graded Exposure:

An introduction is an intellectual conduct treatment practice intended to lessen tension and dread through rehashed contact with what is dreaded. This has been to demonstrate to be among the best medicines that exist for any mental issue. The fundamental hypothesis is that evasion of things we dread outcomes in expanded dread and tension. By methodically moving toward what you may typically stay away from, a noteworthy and enduring decrease in nervousness happens.

Successive Approximation:

A progressive estimate is an intellectual conduct treatment practice that assists individuals with handling troublesome or overpowering objectives. By methodically breaking huge errands into littler advances, or by playing out an assignment like the objective, yet less troublesome, individuals can pick up dominance over the aptitudes expected to accomplish the bigger objective.

Care reflection is an intellectual, social treatment practice that assists individuals with separating from destructive ruminating or fixating, figuring out how to interface with the present minute. Care initially originates from Buddhist contemplation and is the subject of a lot of new research on compelling medications for mental issues.

Intellectual Behavioral Therapy Exercises: Mindfulness Meditation

- Introducing Mindfulness
- Mindfulness 'What' Skills
- Mindfulness 'How' Skills
- Find Wise Mind
- Mindfulness Exercises for Stress Reduction
- Mindfulness Half-Smile Exercise
- Mindfulness Exercises for Chronic Pain

Abilities Training: Skills Training is a subjective social treatment practice intended to cure aptitudes deficiencies, and works through demonstrating direct guidance, and pretends. The most popular subjects of abilities preparing are social aptitudes preparing, confidence preparing, and correspondence preparing.

Psychological Behavioral Therapy Exercises: Social Skills Training

Approving Difficult People

Critical thinking: Problem Solving is a subjective conduct treatment exercise to assist individuals with playing a functioning job in discovering answers for issues. Constant disposition issues or rehashed frustration can bring about individuals playing an uninvolved job when troublesome circumstances emerge. By instructing individuals powerful critical thinking methodologies, they can recover control and make the best of troublesome circumstances.

Unwinding Breathing Training: Relaxation preparing is a subjective social treatment practice intended to assist individuals with decreasing physiological side effects of nervousness, for example, the brevity of breath, quick pulse, wooziness, and so on. By lessening the body's restless excitement, individuals can think all the more unmistakably, in this way expanding sentiments of solace and further diminishing tension manifestations.

CBT has become a novel psychotherapeutic way to deal with treating individuals with psychological well-being issues that underline the centrality of discernment in the assurance of our inclination and conduct. In regular experience, the way we 'outline' a circumstance, whether in positive or negative terms, will decide how we feel about it and how we carry on in it. In CBT, we urge individuals to move our negative musings to grow increasingly adaptable, practically idealistic perspectives about troublesome circumstances. As of late new advancements in CBT emerged from the acknowledgment that only testing our antagonistic considerations is here and there deficient to bring individuals out of discouragement or potentially tension, especially in irreversible circumstances. Acknowledgment and Commitment Therapy (ACT) extends CBT, concentrating on being careful and mindful of our considerations and our association with them to empower ourselves to move toward our most profoundly esteemed qualities in spite of irreversible circumstances or debilitations. ACT depends on the Serenity Prayer: Give me the beauty to acknowledge the things It can't change, to change the things it can, and the intelligence to know the distinction. Keenness is required to consider and withstand life's troubles thoroughly. To see how the centenarians in our investigation managed circumstances that possibly could have 'wrecked them,' we utilized CBT as a hypothetical focal point to investigate their accounts to discover and translate positive methods for being on the planet.

Practically speaking, CB specialists get that while social and logical issues can appear to be overpowering and unsolvable to an individual, close by these unavoidable occasions, there are a few defensive elements to know about when managing customers. In spite of the fact that the '4Ps' model of case definition: inclining, hastening, propagating and defensive components, for this examination, we are keen on defensive variables which are abridged as empowering great associations with family, companions and in a group of friends; abstaining from considering issues to be unendurable; tolerating conditions that can't be changed; moving towards sensible objectives; making an unequivocal move in an unfriendly circumstance; after a misfortune looking approaches to all the more likely comprehend oneself; seeing issues in a more extensive setting; looking after expectation; focusing on one's physical and enthusiastic well-being. The CB specialist concentrated on the psychological and enthusiastic substance of their storylines to build up a psychosocial translation or critique for each.

At the core of CBT is the precept that how we consider things decide how we feel about them, reappraising the significance of a troublesome circumstance with the goal that it is found in progressively positive terms brings about a versatile and flexible reaction. Individuals who normally utilize positive encircling or subjective reappraisal as an instrument to adapt to pressure report more noteworthy mental well-being than the individuals who don't. Numerous individuals consequently ponder a circumstance, making them feel down and on edge and to carry on in manners that are counterproductive to prosperity. The idea record, to assist individuals with testing those negative programmed considerations to land at another option or increasingly adjusted perspective about the circumstance, the cognizant decision to build up a progressively positive illustrative style as a method towards enduring satisfaction. It is illuminating to understand that centenarians had created long-term propensities for positive encircling troublesome circumstances. This capacity placed them in an advantageous position at whatever point life was upsetting.

A strong device utilized by CB specialists is the Worry Tree, where on edge, individuals are approached to see what they are stressing over and afterward to inquire as to whether they can take care of business. On and when the appropriate response is true, at that point, they are told to make an activity arrangement about what to do when to do it, and how to do it. At that point, they are urged to release the stress and change their focal point of consideration. On and when they can't take care of business, at that point, they are urged to release the stress and change their focal point of consideration. We didn't inquire as to whether they had gotten advising in their long lifetime. Clearly naturally, a portion of the centenarians in our examination had gotten this ability in managing pressure. We propose that the successful administration of stress and tension establishes the framework for the capacity to be strong and to bob back despite the pressure.

6 Simple Tips to Cope by Using Cognitive Behavioral Therapy

It's been said that madness is rehashing similar missteps and anticipating various outcomes, but then, after quite a long time after a year, a huge number of individuals all through the world recurrent the regular old examples. They coarseness their teeth and go through the special seasons with guardians who as yet raise the time they were ousted for hitting the instructor with a water expand; in-laws who might condemn every single move each time they see you, and kin who still hold feelings of resentment for since a long time ago overlooked youth battles.

Regularly, these occasions, social affairs imply that there's basically "to an extreme." Individuals eat and drink excessively, overspend, and, when things turn out badly (as they frequently do), it makes a liquefy down circumstance that could have effectively been maintained a strategic distance from. By just applying a couple of strategies that are utilized in intellectual conduct treatment to alter the practices, and evade the triggers, you can transform your family occasions into an increasingly positive, pleasant time.

Psychological Behavioral Therapy (CBT) assists customers with distinguishing their issues and manage their feelings, contemplations, and emotions that impact their conduct or activities. By picking up adapting abilities that CBT educates and afterward applying those aptitudes, individuals can frequently turn those unpleasant family occasions, into positive, cheerful festivals.

In case you're attempting to adapt to an unpleasant family occasion, here are a few thoughts that may divert your family occasions from awful to breathtaking.

Distinguish your triggers and afterward make sense of how to transform them into a positive result.

A model may be a reiteration of the regular old humiliating stories that everybody except you appear to appreciate. So how might you make an alternate situation? Maybe really arranging a family story-time where everybody shares their recollections of a specific time or occurrence. It very well may be amusing, contacting or upbeat, and even an approach to join a family. Another thought is to ask the more seasoned relatives to record their recollections of their adolescence so they can be passed down to the younger ages.

Roll out certain improvements.

On and when your family does likewise a seemingly endless amount of time after a year, maybe weariness has set in. Make a rundown of some positive changes that can be made and propose that they are actualized. Maybe you could change the scene, menu, or even arrangement various exercises that would get the relatives out of their trench.

Forgive and never look back.

Without a doubt, now and then, there will be pressure and strain, however, because somebody proceeds with their conduct, it doesn't imply that you ought to enable them to "bug" you. Some portion of CBT is figuring out how to adapt to circumstances you see as being negative — and if your activities change into a positive (or even impartial) conduct, you'll find that Uncle Joe's comments or even your relative disagreeable snicker don't trouble you so much as it once did.

Offer yourself a reprieve.

This break can be physical, for example, strolling the canine, or mental, for example, 5 minutes alone to unwind with some profound breathing activities. By distinguishing, when your feelings of anxiety are rising hazardously, you can find a way to oversee and decrease them.

Decide to be cheerful.

Your feelings are your decision, and, even though there may be family dramatization in bounty, you don't need to take an interest or enable it to de-rail your state of mind. Avoiding talks that might turn, by remaining occupied and being in the organization of relatives whose organization you appreciate.

Mental fighting (PSYWAR)

Mental fighting (PSYWAR), or the fundamental parts of current mental activities (PSYOP), has been known by numerous different names or terms, including MISO, Psy Ops, political fighting, "Hearts and Minds," and promulgation. The term is utilized "to mean any activity which is rehearsed for the most part by mental strategies with the point of inspiring an arranged mental response in other people#.

Different procedures are utilized, and are planned for impacting an intended interest group's worth framework, conviction framework, feelings, thought processes, thinking, or conduct. It is utilized to initiate admissions or strengthen dispositions and practices ideal to the originator's destinations, and are here and there joined with dark activities or bogus banner strategies. It is additionally used to pulverize the confidence of foes through strategies that expect to discourage troops' mental states.

Target spectators can be governments, associations, gatherings, and people, and isn't simply restricted to officers. Regular people of remote regions can likewise be focused by innovation and media to cause an impact in the administration of their nation.

In Propaganda: The Formation of Men's Attitudes, mental fighting as a typical harmony strategy practice between countries as a type of backhanded hostility. This kind of purposeful publicity depletes the general assessment of a restricting system by stripping its capacity ceaselessly on popular sentiment. This type of animosity is difficult to shield against because no universal courtroom is fit for ensuring against mental hostility since it can't be legitimately arbitrated. "Here, the proselytizers are managing an outside foe whose resolve he looks to wreck by mental implies with the goal that the adversary starts to question the legitimacy of his convictions and activities.

There is proof of mental fighting all through recorded history. In current occasions, mental fighting endeavors have been utilized widely. Mass correspondence takes into consideration direct correspondence with an adversary people and subsequently has been utilized in numerous endeavors. As of late, the web takes into consideration battles of disinformation and falsehood performed by operators anyplace on the planet.

CHAPTER SEVEN

USING NEUROLINGUISTIC PROGRAMMING (NLP) TO INFLUENCE PEOPLE

Neuro-Linguistic Programming, or NLP, is the procedure by which the human personality makes a reality dependent on tactile info, sentiments, and language that is then placed into perceptible examples. These examples are then utilized by the intuitive to decide how an individual ought to react to circumstances physically and inwardly.

Having a cognizant familiarity with this procedure enables an individual to make their world. At first, this may sound somewhat shocking to the easygoing onlooker; anyway, its reason depends on science as we become increasingly acquainted with how the human personality works. At the point when somebody gets oneself in a circumstance that may not be bringing the ideal outcomes, the capacity to change the result in a moment is an incredible asset.

Illustrative frameworks depend on the faculties and how every individual likes to acclimatize and process new data. Some want to imagine it, some need to talk about it, and others may need to "feel" it. Contingent upon an individual's favored authentic style, managing them in that equivalent style may influence them in your mind. You are imparting a similar idea or thought; however, you are doing it, so that sounds good to them.

Very much framed results are actualized by plainly characterizing the ideal results and positively expressing them. As opposed to stating what you don't need, unmistakably state what you do need. When you have your ideal outcomes unmistakably characterized, you'll have to give the thought setting through envisioning the result with the related physical things you may understand. For instance, you need to imagine the sound of someone's voice, the encompassing commotion you would hope to hear, or any scents or different things you may encounter once the objective is accomplished.

Imparting the result to others as such enables them to see the profit and can carry them in your mind. Making your ideal result, convincing enough to others, will give them the longing to accomplish a similar objective. Numerous publicists utilize this representation to allure clients to purchase their items by portraying what their life would resemble on and when they obtained a specific item. This representation encourages the client to "see" the objective of a glad life.

Displaying greatness is another system utilized under the NLP umbrella. By demonstrating yourself on a fruitful individual, or reflecting another person who has had an achievement, you are taking on their conviction framework and their world. You likewise increase extra understanding into why they settle on the choices they do and how their convictions impact the decisions they make. When addressing somebody utilizing their conviction framework, you are bound to persuade them regarding the legitimacy of your contemplations and thoughts.

These strategies can be applied to numerous circumstances and are progressively being used in the business world. How effective do you figure an individual could become if they could legitimately impact the activities of their colleagues? Having the option to impact everyone around you isn't really a type of control yet cooperative energy of sorts that enables people to push ahead on the whole with one reason. Having everybody in agreement and without singular wants at the top of the priority list implies that the result is bound to be agreeable to everybody

NLP has numerous utilizations in business, and one of the key uses is to pick up impact over other individuals. How might you want to have the option to impart in a manner that empowered you to effortlessly communicate as the need should arise to individuals at all various degrees of an association? How might you want to have the option to persuade somebody to accomplish something just by your utilization of explicit language designs? How might you want to have the option to assist individuals with conquering their issues to make them progressively effective and profitable? How might you like to have the option to impact client decisions by speaking with them at an oblivious level, so that they simply get a positive sentiment about your item or support and acknowledge your recommendations?

NLP Communication Model

How can it work? All things considered, NLP instructs you that we, as a whole, have individual inclinations by the way we think, how we speak to the world to ourselves. On and when we can comprehend how that we figure, at that point, we can impact how we think.

For instance, we, as a whole, have a favored framework for deciphering what goes on in our lives into our musings. We either like to utilize our feeling of sight, sound, or contact. If we have a favored feeling of sight, at that point, we will interpret effectively what we experience into pictures in our minds. On and when we have a favored feeling of touch, at that point, we will effortlessly interpret that into interior emotions and so forth.

Let' s state that we incline to sight or pictures. This will get clear in addition to other things in the things that we state, "see you later," "I can see that event," "Out of the picture and therefore irrelevant," and so forth. All expressions that include the feeling of sight.

When we incline contact, at that point, we may make statements like "look you up some other time," "you can clutch that idea," "I get a positive sentiment when I think about that," all expressions that include a physical feeling of touch or feeling.

Thus, if we know this, at that point, we can tune in to what individuals state, and we can determine what their favored vehicle of correspondence is. We can increase the oblivious impact over them by utilizing their favored arrangement of correspondence back to them. Thus, we will utilize words and expressions that they use to do this.

Have you seen that individuals like individuals who resemble them? Do you and your companions have normal interests? This is how it works.

Give this a shot next time you are conversing with them. Watch their shoulders go here and there as they breathe in and out, and duplicate them. In this way, when they breathe in, you breathe in, when they breathe out, you breath out. Notice how it gives you an oblivious association with them. They won't realize what you have done; however, they will feel progressively associated with them, and they will like you all the more subliminally.

One of the significant commitments NLP has made to self-awareness, and life improvement is its applications to correspondence both inside and outside. NLP offers numerous functional methods to enable us to participate in increasingly important cooperations with people around us by constraining a significant number of the hindrances to viable correspondence. This article will take a gander at a portion of the manners in which NLP can improve our relational abilities explicitly with others, and in doing so, upgrade the nature of our lives.

Called Neuro-Linguistic programming for an explanation, NLP is centered around the language designs associated with how we speak with ourselves as well as other people. Language designs, explicitly the words we use and how we use them profoundly affect our experience of consistent life. At the point when we have an encounter of any sort, at that point, we give a mark to that understanding, the name, or the words we use BECOME the experience. For instance, you come back from a day at Disneyland, and somebody asks you how it was. You may answer it was wonderful, fabulous, exciting, startling, energizing, fun, heart siphoning or insane... whichever word you decide to depict the experience, IS the experience. Let's assume you picked 'frightening.' Extremely the word 'frightening' is nothing, and it's only a mix of letters. And yet startling is a believing, a lot of contemplations and mental symbolism that is related to that blend of letters. Think about this: Imagine on and when you didn't have a clue about the word startling? For reasons unknown, it had been overlooked from your jargon, or you'd never heard it said as a kid. OK, realize that how will generally be 'terrified'? It's accounted for that some little island countries don't have a word for 'war'... Envision how that influences their lifestyle!

Words cause compound responses in our brains. The things we state or hear said to us, especially the words that they are said in, cause us to feel certain ways about things and respond in specific manners to specific conditions.

How would you answer when somebody asks, "How are you?"? Do you carelessly answer "Fine" or "alright." How would you feel when you state that? How would you feel after you have said it?

Imagine a scenario where you answered, "Remarkable!" "Extremely Superb," or "Awesome. Do you figure you would feel unexpectedly? Two individuals can have similar encounters every day, except one can mark them "alright," and one can call them "Great," and as an outcome, one individual will FEEL wonderful, and one will physically feel OK.

Do you see the intensity of words yet?

If not, consider it in a progressively outside correspondence typesetting. Let's assume somebody has recently given you their feeling on something and you answer "I don't know I agree"... Do you figure this would make the individual feel distinctively on, and when you said: "You're WRONG." The two answers have demonstrated similar importance... you don't concur with them, yet the words utilized make significantly various responses thus enormously impact the connection between the two individuals. Alright, OK, you get it; words impact how we feel.

As a Life mentor and NLP ace specialist. NLP is a ground-breaking technique that can assist you in getting the outcomes you need in all aspects of your life. By utilizing the accompanying procedure, you will have the option to tweak your objectives, find what you truly need, and the means, to accomplish it!

1. Positive

What do you need? This must be expressed in the positive as your subliminal personality doesn't have the foggiest idea about the contrast among constructive and contrary

Did you realize that residence in the negative can really be awful for your wellbeing!

2. Tangible explicit

By what method will you know when you have it?

What will you do when you get it?

What will you see, hear, and feel like when you have it?

3. Contextualized

Where and when would you like to have it?

Where and when do you not need it?

4. Self-attainable

Significantly, the objective must be inside your very own domain of impact, for example, is something you have control over.

What assets do you have the option to accomplish?

What do you have to do to accomplish it?

Is this something which you, yourself, can accomplish? Or, then again, does it necessitate that other individuals carry on with a specific goal in mind?

5. Natural

What are the favorable circumstances and weaknesses? There are consistently inconveniences in rolling out an improvement - being aware of these keeps you 'at cause' by settling on it your decision.

What are the upsides of rolling out this improvement?

What are the disservices of rolling out this improvement?

What will accomplishing this cost you? Become?

6. Beneficial

This is the inspiration question. Which of your qualities will be satisfied by accomplishing this objective?

What's critical to you about getting it?

What will this objective assist you with abstaining from feeling?

What is the advantage of this objective?

7. The initial step

Do you have an initial step? To transform your fantasy into a solid reality, you pole venture out; without it, you won't gather up adequate speed to take you the following stride.

Use NLP to Create Changes and Shifts for Others During Ordinary Conversations

Discussing successfully with other individuals is a fundamental ability that a couple is extremely ready to accomplish. Since individuals learn and process data in an unexpected way, your style may not concur with the individual you're addressing. This dissimilarity in correspondence styles regularly prompts mistaken assumptions and hard emotions.

Consider the possibility that you could quickly set up an affinity with anybody. On and when you right now feel cumbersome when meeting new individuals, you are not conveying viably and could be losing commonly compensating connections. The capacity to make an association with somebody finishes you pretty much every part of your life. Personal, business, and easygoing connections are altogether affected by your capacity to enough convey in a way that is effectively comprehended and generally welcomed.

NLP offers a few procedures that enable you to express what is on your mind just as to comfort the other party. If they are from a casual perspective, they will be increasingly open to your thoughts and perspectives.

Animals in the normal world do almost no correspondence through vocal language. Just individuals depend exclusively on the expressed word to demonstrate our contemplations, emotions, thoughts, and by and large perspective. While watching other living things, it turns out to be very evident that a discussion is going on that we don't hear yet that they unmistakably get it. Not clear to most people, we also have an implicit exchange that we use to convey our perspective to other people, what we know as non-verbal communication is frequently disregarded or not taken note. NLP utilizes this implicit language now and again to build up affinity and a feeling of recognition.

This is accomplished by discreetly watching the non-verbal communication of the other individual. When you get a feeling of their stance, characteristics, and manner of speaking, you can start the way toward coordinating and reflecting these practices. There is inquire about that emphatically proposes we like individuals who are most similar to us. By imitating the conduct of another person, you are comforting that person and making the person in question increasingly responsive to loosened up discussion. Along these lines, they will tune in to what you need to state with a receptive outlook and can be emphatically impacted.

Implanted directions are questions that lead with a recommendation of an idea or thought that, at that point, becomes planted in the audience member's mind. An inquiry that starts with "What might it be like..." makes the audience picture their answer before vocalizing it. Giving an idea setting makes it a reality, and by posing these sorts of inquiries, you are giving your audience another reality and changing their conviction framework.

Although NLP could be viewed as a training that is utilized for control and control, it ought to be utilized as a positive impact for you and your general surroundings. At the point when utilized in a valuable way, NLP can decidedly change your world and the truth of others that you come into contact with regularly. This positive impact reduces strife and fortifies connections.

CHAPTER SEVEN

USING COGNITIVE BEHAVIOURAL THERAPY (CBT) TO INFLUENCE PEOPLE

Psychological conduct treatment (CBT) is a sort of psychotherapeutic treatment that assists patients with understanding the musings and emotions that impact practices. CBT is ordinarily used to treat a wide scope of disarranges, including fears, addictions, sadness, and nervousness.

Intellectual conduct treatment is commonly present moment and concentrated on helping customers manage a quite specific issue. Throughout the treatment, individuals figure out how to recognize and change ruinous or upsetting idea designs that impact conduct and feelings.

Subjective Behavioral Therapy Basics

The hidden idea that is driving CBT is that our considerations and sentiments assume a key job in our conduct. For instance, an individual who invests a great deal of energy considering plane accidents, runway mishaps, and other air catastrophes may end up maintaining a strategic distance from air travel.

The objective of subjective conduct treatment is to instruct patients that while they can't control each part of their general surroundings, they can assume responsibility for how they decipher and manage things in their condition.

Subjective conduct treatment has gotten progressively mainstream as of late with both emotional well-being shoppers and treatment experts. Since CBT is normally a transient treatment alternative, it is frequently more reasonable than some different sorts of treatment. CBT is additionally experimentally bolstered and has been appeared to successfully assist patients with conquering a wide assortment of maladaptive practices.

Programmed Negative Thoughts

One of the primary focal points of intellectual conduct treatment is on changing the programmed negative musings that can add to and worsen enthusiastic troubles, despondency, and uneasiness. These negative musings spring forward suddenly, are acknowledged as obvious, and will, in general, contrarily impact the person's state of mind.

Through the CBT procedure, patients inspect these contemplations and are urged to take a gander at the proof from reality that either underpins or invalidates these considerations. By doing this, individuals can take a progressively objective and sensible take a gander at the contemplations that add to their sentiments of tension and sadness. By getting mindful of the contrary and frequently unreasonable contemplations that hose their sentiments and dispositions, individuals can begin participating in more advantageous reasoning patterns.2

Kinds of Cognitive Behavior Therapy

Social and Cognitive Psychotherapies, "Intellectual and conduct psychotherapies are a scope of treatments dependent on ideas and standards got from mental models of human feeling and conduct. They incorporate a wide scope of treatment approaches for an enthusiastic issue, along a continuum from organized individual psychotherapy to self-improvement material."

There are various explicit kinds of restorative methodologies that include CBT that are normally utilized by psychological wellness experts. Instances of these include:

- Rational Emotive Behavior Therapy (REBT): This sort of CBT is fixated on distinguishing and adjusting unreasonable convictions. The procedure of REBT includes distinguishing the fundamental nonsensical convictions, effectively testing these convictions, lastly figuring out how to perceive and change these idea designs.

- Cognitive Therapy: This type of treatment is focused on distinguishing and changing off base or mutilated reasoning examples, enthusiastic reactions, and behaviors.3

- Multimodal Therapy: This type of CBT recommends that mental issues must be treated by tending to seven distinctive yet interconnected modalities, which are conduct, influence, sensation, symbolism, perception, relational factors, and medication or natural considerations.4

- Dialectical Behavior Therapy: This kind of subjective social treatment tends to intuition examples and practices and consolidates systems, for example, passionate guidelines and care.

While each sort of subjective social treatment offers its very own exceptional methodology, every middle on tending to the basic idea designs that add to mental pain.

The Components of Cognitive Behavior Therapy

Individuals regularly experience musings or emotions that strengthen or compound broken convictions. Such convictions can bring about risky practices that can influence various life territories, including family, sentimental connections, work, and scholastics.

For instance, an individual experiencing low confidence may encounter negative musings about their very own capacities or appearance. Because of these negative reasoning examples, the individual may begin maintaining a strategic distance from social circumstances or leave behind open doors for progression at work or school.

To battle these damaging considerations and practices, a psychological conduct advisor starts by helping the customer to recognize the dangerous convictions. This stage, known as useful investigation, is significant for figuring out how contemplations, emotions, and circumstances can add to maladaptive behaviors.5 The procedure can be troublesome, particularly for patients who battle with reflection, yet it can eventually prompt self-disclosure and bits of knowledge that are a basic piece of the treatment procedure.

The second piece of subjective conduct treatment centers around the genuine practices that are adding to the issue. The customer starts to learn and rehearse new aptitudes that would then be able to be placed in to use in genuine circumstances. For instance, an individual experiencing illicit drug use may begin rehearsing new adapting abilities and practicing approaches to maintain a strategic distance from or manage social circumstances that might trigger a backslide.

As a rule, CBT is a progressive procedure that enables an individual to make steady strides towards a conduct change. Somebody experiencing social nervousness may begin by essentially envisioning himself in a tension inciting social circumstances.

Next, the customer may begin rehearsing discussions with companions, family, and colleagues. By dynamically progressing in the direction of a bigger objective, the procedure appears to be less overwhelming and the objectives simpler to accomplish.

The Process of Cognitive Behavior Therapy

- During the procedure of CBT, the advisor will, in general, play an extremely dynamic job.
- CBT is exceptionally objective arranged and centered, and the customer and specialist cooperate as associates toward the commonly settled objectives.
- The advisor will regularly clarify the procedure in detail, and the customer will frequently be offered schoolwork to finish between sessions.
- Cognitive-conduct treatment can be successfully utilized as a momentary treatment focused on helping the customer manage a quite specific problem.2

Employments of Cognitive Behavior Therapy

Subjective conduct treatment has been utilized to treat individuals experiencing a wide scope of disarranges, including:

- Anxiety
- Phobias

- Depression

- Addictions

- Eating issue

- Panic assaults

- Anger

CBT is one of the most explored kinds of treatment, to some extent, since treatment is centered around profoundly explicit objectives, and results can be estimated moderately effectively.

Contrasted with psychoanalytic sorts of psychotherapy which support a progressively open-finished self-investigation, psychological conduct treatment is frequently most appropriate for customers who are increasingly alright with an organized and centered methodology in which the advisor regularly plays an instructional job. Be that as it may, for CBT to be successful, the individual must be prepared and ready to invest energy and exertion investigating their contemplations and emotions. Such self-investigation and schoolwork can be troublesome; however, it is an incredible method to become familiar with how inward states sway outward conduct.

Intellectual conduct treatment is additionally appropriate for individuals searching for a momentary treatment choice for particular kinds of passionate trouble that doesn't include psychotropic medicine. Probably the best advantage of psychological conduct treatment is that it assists customers with creating adapting aptitudes that can be helpful both now and later on.

CBT joins psychological treatment and conduct treatment

CBT centers around changing unhelpful or undesirable considerations and practices. It is a mix of two treatments: 'intellectual treatment' and 'conduct treatment.' The premise of both these methods is that sound contemplations lead to solid emotions and practices.

Subjective treatment

The point of subjective treatment is to change how an individual ponders an issue that is causing concern. Negative contemplations cause pointless emotions and practices. For instance, somebody who thinks they are contemptible of affection or regard may feel pulled back in social circumstances and act modestly. Intellectual treatment challenges those considerations and furnishes the individual with more beneficial procedures.

Numerous methods are accessible. One method includes requesting that the individual thinks of proof to 'demonstrate' that they are unlovable. This may incorporate provoking the individual to recognize the loved ones who love and regard them. This proof causes the individual to understand that their conviction is bogus. This is called 'subjective rebuilding.' The individual figures out how to recognize and challenge negative musings and supplant them with progressively sensible and positive contemplations.

Conduct treatment

The point of conduct treatment is to show the individual systems or abilities to change their conduct. For instance, an individual who carries on timidly at a gathering may have negative contemplations and emotions about themselves. They may likewise need social abilities.

Conduct treatment shows the individual increasingly accommodating practices. For instance, they might be shown conversational abilities that they practice in treatment and social circumstances. Adverse contemplations and sentiments lessen as the individual finds they can have a good time in social circumstances.

Treatment with CBT

The subtleties of treatment will change as per the individual's concern. Notwithstanding, CBT commonly incorporates the accompanying:

- Assessment – this may incorporate rounding out polls to assist you with portraying your specific issue and pinpoint troubling side effects. You will be approached to finish frames now and then with the goal that you and your advisor can plot your advance and recognize issues or manifestations that need additional consideration

- Personal training – your specialist gives composed materials (for example, handouts or books) to assist you with getting familiar with your specific issue. The idiom 'information is control' is a foundation of CBT. A decent comprehension of your specific mental issue will assist you with dismissing unwarranted apprehensions, which will facilitate your nervousness and other negative sentiments

- Goal setting – your specialist, causes you to draw up a rundown of objectives you wish to accomplish from treatment (for instance, you might need to defeat your bashfulness in social settings). You and your specialist work out handy methodologies to help satisfy these objectives

- The practice of procedures – you practice your new systems with the specialist. For instance, you may pretend troublesome social circumstances or practical self-talk (how you converse with yourself in your mind) to supplant undesirable or negative self-talk

- Homework – you will be relied upon to take an interest in your very own treatment effectively. You are urged to utilize the viable procedures you have worked on throughout your day by day life and report the outcomes to the specialist. For instance, the advisor may request that you keep a journal.

CBT and drug

The drug isn't always required. CBT can be as powerful as medicine in the treatment of sorrow and uneasiness. In different cases, you and your advisor may choose that medicine, together with CBT, would deliver the best outcomes. For instance, individuals with a bipolar issue, for the most part, profit by prescription that helps control their emotional episodes.

CHAPTER EIGHT

THE EFFECTIVE USE OF PERSUASION, MANIPULATION, AND DECEPTION

8 Simple Techniques to Persuade and Influence People

1. Confining

This strategy is frequently utilized in legislative issues. The most prevalent case of confining is the legacy charge. Lawmakers restricted to this expense will call it "demise charge." The utilization of "death" rather than "legacy" causes a wide range of undesirable affiliations.

Confining is a genuinely unpretentious system, yet utilizing emotive words, for example, "passing," you will have more opportunities to persuade individuals to acknowledge your perspective.

2. Reflection

This is a mainstream system utilized in NLP. Reflecting somebody implies copying his developments. Developments can be practically vague; however, the most evident of them are the hand signals, inclining forward or in reverse, different developments of the head or hands. We as a whole do it unknowingly, and on and when you look carefully, you may see it.

The best approach to reflect somebody abandons saying. Notwithstanding, there are a couple of proposals: Try to do it intangibly, and do an interim of 2-4 seconds between the developments of the individual and your appearance.

3. Shortfall

Promoters frequently utilize this procedure. Openings, whatever they might be, draw in unmistakably more on and when we confine access to them.

This strategy can be effectively applied to any individual in an appropriate circumstance. Be that as it may, all the more critically, the information on this strategy will make you remain wary. Stop and consider how the way influences you that the amount of merchandise is constrained. On and when the item is constrained, at that point, there must be an enormous interest for it, isn't that so?

4. Exchange

At the point when somebody causes us or accomplishes something pleasant for us, we feel constrained to pay him back. In this manner, on and when you need somebody to accomplish something for you, why not to accomplish something for him first? Regardless of where or when you do it (with your colleagues or with your neighbor), the primary concern is to step up to the plate.

5. Timing

Generally, individuals are increasingly accommodating and adaptable when they are rationally worn out. Before you get some information about something, attempt to await a chance until that individual accomplishes something that requires impressive mental exertion, you can get your associate in transit out toward the day's end, and regardless of what you requested, doubtlessly, he will say: "I'll do it tomorrow."

6. Coinciding

We, as a whole, intuitively attempt to act reliably. One of the genuine models is a method utilized by merchants. A merchant shakes your hand while you are arranging the buy. The vast majority partner handshaking with the consummation of the exchange. In this manner, making it before the arrangement was finished, the merchant has more opportunities to cause you to concur.

A decent method to utilize this technique is to convince individuals to make a move before the coherent personality turns on. For instance, on and when you stroll with a companion and need to head out to see a film, yet he or she isn't certain about that, you can go towards the film until he or she chooses.

Step by step instructions to impact individuals with NLP

The moral utilization of NLP impact when instructing customers

As an NLP Practitioner and Hypnotherapist, once in a while, people anticipate that I should do a wide range of Derren Brown-like stuff on them, making them give me their wallets or convincing them to get things done without wanting to.

While the information on NLP (Neuro-Linguistic Programming) and mesmerizing can undoubtedly be utilized for growing progressively successful messages, I imagine that individuals who use it with expectations of causing everybody to do what they state have sort of overlooked the main issue.

The purpose of learning NLP for me was to have the option to comprehend individuals more, to recognize how they work, and to meet them where they are.

It has instructed me to regard individuals' points of view, their encounters, and to open my brain to their method for seeing the world.

As a result of getting individuals, I normally find that individuals are all the more ready to tune in to what I need to state. Since they feel comprehended, regarded, and tuned in to. Now and again, that is a cognizant thing, and once in a while, it is a totally oblivious procedure, and they don't have the foggiest idea why they trust me; however, they do.

Trust is the foundation of influence - if you are carrying on dishonesty, eventually, you will meet a clingy end.

If you can collect trust from individuals, they are bound to need to conform to your solicitations instead of you practicing some otherworldly Ming-like control over them, convincing them to make your offering.

Generally, NLP is about sympathy and getting individuals. It can likewise be utilized to assist individuals with picking another method for taking a gander at the world. In any case, to do that, you need to have the option to comprehend what they are accustomed to on the planet. Regard that first, show you comprehend, and at precisely that point, individuals can be guided by you to settle on increasingly valuable choices.

Influence - Logic and Reason Require

What strikes a chord when you hear the word Persuasion? To some, it evokes doubt, double-dealing, and control. The outcome can be to delude or degenerate the brain of the individuals who are effectively overwhelmed.

For some, this makes shut personalities any and numerous new contemplations. If you figure this doesn't concern you, at that point, pose this inquiry: Are you particular about what you will consider or tune in to? Exactly how high are your psychological spam channels set?

All things considered, what is your opinion about MLM's (staggered or organize promoting)?

If it's not too much trouble note... this isn't an article about MLM's.

Did you realize that MLM's have developed and there is really a third era of MLM that even Blue Chip Corporations are utilizing? A few gauges for the following decade anticipate 70% of items will be accessible by direct showcasing.

If you didn't have a clue about this, why? Would it be able to be because you were shut disapproved?

If you are shut disapproved, at that point, be guaranteed that you're some in your group of spectators will as well. Influence is a fundamental need in discourse to conquer the crowd esteems and outlook if they are shut. Influential talking and the craft of influence are basic aptitudes.

So, where does influence fit into open talking?
To comprehend the appropriate response, it may be a great idea to return to the beginnings of formal open talking. How about we

return to antiquated Greece. In layman's Greek, the word convinces in a positive sense would intend to persuade, to change the psyches of audience members by methods for coherent ideas and sound thinking.

So an open speaker needs to persuade, to change the psyches of a crowd of people with coherent ideas and sound thinking. In what manner would this be able to be practiced in your discourse?

If you are going to change the psyche of your group of spectators or convince them, think about these zones of study.

Your Audience would be the principal thought. What are their considerations regarding the matter? Testing of the group of spectators will be essential to realize how to continue.

For example, MLM's, have any been engaged with them? Have any been singed or squandered cash on them? Have any benefitted from them? These inquiries can be changed to your convincing subject.

What will be the makeup of the group of spectators? Extra look into how to address these gatherings will be gainful. Catchphrases to gaze upward would be...

- Grown-up Audience

- Develop Audience

- Youthful Audiences

When the group of spectators is characterized, it will be imperative to know their qualities. This is a crucial thought before setting up the introduction. By what means will you discover the contemplations and estimations of the group of spectators? You should become more acquainted with the...

Group of spectators Professed Values

Convincing open talking, to be viable, should be mindful of the necessities and the contemplations of the group of spectators.

Posing Inquiries will be the following assignment to improve your tuning in. The craft of posing inquiries will likewise assist you in knowing how to plan to convince best.

Thinking will be straightaway. To persuade or change the brain with a coherent idea and sound thinking will bring about influence.

Argumentation can be a viable method to reason. Keep in mind you should be careful. At the point when a cruising vessel needs to conflict with the breeze, it doesn't take it head-on. It is called attaching. Speakers need to utilize respect likewise.

Did you see next to no here is tied in with thinking, rationale, and evolving minds? That is because they are the simple part. The crucial step of this is interfacing with a group of spectators. The test is to get into their reasoning.

Dissuading Reasonableness

When attempting to convince, reason with a similar sensibility that you would hope to appear, many will be killed and have left thinking that this is some sort of pitch. Did you have an awkward inclination by then? What contemplations did you have when you continued perusing?

Keep in mind that Feeling to Master Persuasion

Keep in mind that feeling whenever you need to convince somebody. They have forceful feelings and sentiments that you may need to get around carefully. Similarly, as that cruising ship needs to attach to gain forward ground, in like manner, you should utilize politeness while convincing. Convince with a sensibility as you present your sound rationale.

Get familiar with the Art of Positive Persuasion

Keep in mind, if you need to be fruitful in deals, you have to consistently have your customers and prospects wellbeing on a basic level. That implies you can never prevail in deals in the long haul, on and when you attempt to control or pressure individuals, as opposed to impact them emphatically.

Understanding the Concept of Positive Influence and Persuasion

As a beginning stage, it is important to comprehend that to decidedly impact anybody; you have to comprehend that there are three separate parts to influence.

Rationale

The first requires the utilization of rationale for example this is where you totally comprehend your item or administration incentive; you have distinguished the ideal client, who needs precisely what you bring to the table. At that point utilizing this data to illuminate them, you enable them to utilize their rationale to arrive at a positive resolution, in which they comprehend your incentive entirely, and they see that it addresses or surpasses their issues and desires.

Feeling

As you most likely are aware individuals purchase with their feelings, so you must comprehend this pivotal component in the influence procedure. This is the piece of the business procedure where you have clarified, and your customer has seen all the intelligent reasons why your item or administration is the best choice accessible to them. At this stage, they comprehend your incentive entirely, from a coherent planned. Your job now as a business proficient is to interest your client's certain feelings, with the goal that they can totally comprehend, "How might this benefit them."

The positive feelings alluding to here are satisfaction, satisfaction, important commitment, acknowledgment, love, empathy, respect, and pride. To make this piece of the business procedure work for you, you should totally comprehend your incentive and every one of the advantages it offers your client. Utilizing this as the beginning stage, reveal how your client will profit by utilizing your item or support and depict this to them from an emotive viewpoint.

Activity Idea: Explore the positive feelings depicted above in intense Italic; presently analyze your item or administration benefits. Connection, your clients, need to at least one of the advantages your item offers and portray this to them, as far as one of the positive feelings they will understanding, because of utilizing your item or administration.

Morals

The last machine gear-piece in the wheel of positive influence is uprightness, consistency, and great character. Fundamentally what this way to any great deals proficient is that they should consistently be credible, 100 % fair, and accept totally in what they need to sell. The really extraordinary deals proficient doesn't just have faith in what they sell, and what they do; however, they are a living case of it. Their activities, words, and deeds epitomize all that they represent. As it were on and when you need to be an extraordinary deal proficient, you should walk your discussion. Be the model that you need the world to reflect to you.

You can never endeavor to convince anybody if you are not decidedly convinced yourself emphatically. Similarly, as you could never request that somebody accomplishes something you never have or could never do, you can never manufacture a commonly advantageous long haul deals association with anybody; if you are endeavoring to sell something, you would not happily get yourself. Your clients will see directly through you if you demonstration in-truly or on, and when you attempt to sell them something, you don't have faith in 100 % yourself. Individuals are extremely responsive to emotions, and they will effortlessly see your negative sentiments towards your item, either in your words or non-verbal communication.

Influence is Never Trickery or Deception

The key chief to be compelling when decidedly impacting individuals is to be 100 % credible and yourself. Individuals will see directly through you if you attempt to be somebody else. Being genuine and moral, when convincing individuals is the careful inverse of control. At the point when you are a living case of your attempt to sell something and individuals can see that you have their eventual benefits on the most fundamental level, they will rapidly be warm to you and enthusiastically structure long haul commonly valuable associations with you. What are you sitting tight for? Be true and moral, and you will open the conduits on your business achievement this year.

CHAPTER NINE

TIPS TO NEUROLINGUISTICS PROGRAMMING

Neuro-Linguistic Programming, or NLP, gives handy manners by which you can change how you think, see past occasions, and approach your life.

Neuro-Linguistic Programming tells you the best way to assume responsibility for your psyche, and in this way, your life. In contrast to therapy, which centers around the 'why,' NLP is commonsense and centers around the 'how.'

5 Tips to Improve Your NLP Practitioner Skills

The NLP Practitioner preparing has such a large number of methods and devices fused that you truly could spend a lifetime sharpening your capacities. After numerous years in the realm of NLP, both as an instructor and mentor, I end up revealing layer after layer about how various systems can be joined, how to show signs of improvement or quicker results, and enhancing my very own structures. I understand that among the perusers of this blog there are the individuals who are as of late authorized as NLP Practitioners, and the individuals who are knowledgeable about the field, so I have deliberately picked the accompanying tips:

1. Build up Your Sensory Acuity

As the vast majority of us need to accomplish the hot examples and language aptitudes, we saw our coaches do and we so delightfully working on, building up your capacity to really see what is happening might be effectively overlooked. Be that as it may, with an excellent tangible keenness, you will find that the aftereffects of your work will improve significantly. The more you can see state moves in your customers, adjust, and see the non-verbals, the more fruitful you will be. Connection creates tactile keenness. Or then again compose the article.

2. Re-center around your Milton Model

The Milton Model has such a large number of components to it that you will undoubtedly have the option to improve something in your range of abilities. I suggest checking on your NLP Practitioner manual for the Milton Model segment and see which component merits center. Practice it! Maybe 10 minutes every day, while in transit to work, or by composing with a whiteboard marker on your restroom reflect.

3. Give Your Work with Submodalities a Little More Umpf

Audit every one of those points canvassed in your NLP Practitioner preparing that secured Submodalities. An inquiry to pose to yourself is, "can you rapidly whip out all the distinctive submodalities that are there that you could approach a customer for?" And provided that this is true, how might you get truly inventive when making new examples of your own at a further developed level by joining various types of submodality designs?

4. Spot Yourself Out of Your Comfort Zone

A large portion of us floats towards a specific part of NLP, applying certain systems more than others. The guideline of stretch, particularly for the more cultivated NLP Practitioner. Working inside

70% of your customary range of familiarity and 30% out of your usual range of familiarity will keep you large and in charge when working with others. The 30% is the place learning happens, so if you have been staying away from, for example, tying down, feel free to grapple away!NLP Practitioner Miami.

5. Apply NLP on Yourself Daily

A few of us may neglect to apply our NLP aptitudes on ourselves day by day intentionally. As an NLP Practitioner, significantly, we continue utilizing the instruments and various systems on ourselves. We will effortlessly turn out to be unknowingly capable, yet there are typically a few apparatuses with which we are still at the degree of intentionally skillful.

Top 10 hints and deceives for an NLP Beginner

The philosophy of NLP alongside the entirety of the systems and examples lead to a colossal measure of data and abilities that are accessible to the NLP fledgling. Here are a couple of tips and deceives from my understanding to make this learning task sensible, however charming!

1. Lump down – Even only one bit of NLP, for example, the meta-model can be overpowering if you endeavor to ace the entire range of abilities without a moment's delay. The primary errand in any huge learning process is to separate it into sensible lumps. Here is the test: if the piece that you are thinking about learning overpowers you, separate it into its part pieces and start with one of those first! You can't eat a whole elephant in one chomp, can you?

2. Organize – If the pieces are suitably measured regardless of you feel overpowered, it is no doubt an issue of prioritization and sequencing. When your learning errands are a sensible lump size, ask yourself inquiries, for example, "What piece, on and when I learn it currently, will make learning different pieces simpler?", "What is the most significant piece, that on and when I center around it first, will have the most effect on my life?" or "Which piece will I have a ton of fun with today!"

3. Activity, Action, Action – Reading is pleasant; however, there is a major contrast between viable understanding and successful activity. Get out on the planet and use it! Careful discipline brings about promising results. Would you like to be an ace peruser or an ace Practitioner?

4. Apply to self – Upon completing NLP preparing, it is my experience that understudies will, in general, become best at the methods that have had the most effect without anyone else lives. Encountering it yourself gives you a lot more extravagant comprehension of the devices and their impacts than utilizing them on others. Also, by not utilizing such an integral asset set on yourself, you are passing up the individual change that can take your aptitudes to the following level!

5. Make a day by day schedule – Make it a propensity to rehearse day by day, regardless of whether just quickly. After procuring new abilities, you will start to see new chances to rehearse. Use them!

6. There is nothing of the sort as a disappointment, just Feedback!! Use criticism astutely to recognize what your subsequent stage for development is, and consistently make sure to commend your accomplishments!

7. You, as of now, have the entirety of the assets you need – When you acknowledge and acknowledge where you are in the learning procedure, learning comes all the more effectively, and the adventure that you are on turns out to be

significantly more lovely. Achievement isn't a goal; it is a voyage.

8. Be available to see what we call NLP in its normally happening condition. Greatness exists once in a while in the most bizarre of spots, and you can generally gain from seeing greatness in its normal setting. Where do you think NLP originated from in any case!

9. Practice, practice, and practice some more.

10. Have a great time!! Individuals find out increasingly, snappier, and keep up learning over a more drawn out timeframe when they are having some good times. They additionally have some good times simultaneously! Appears to be a success win for me!

Neurolinguistic Programming Tutorial

A fundamental NLP instructional exercise will be introduced in this article to give more knowledge into this regularly talked about, however minimal comprehended, a subcategory of brain research. Usually, NLP is mistaken for mesmerizing, yet they are in certainty unique, although both can be applied in comparative manners, and would they be able to supplement each other well. After this short article, you'll have significantly more knowledge of what its center truly is.

To start with, NLP, which represents neuro phonetic writing computer programs, was established by two men, John Grinder and Richard Bandler, during the 1970s. They authored the term to indicate their faith in a nexus between neurological procedure, language, and examples of conduct that have been adapted, however, understanding, and that be composed to arrive at explicit objectives throughout everyday life.

Some individuals are particularly skilled at what they do. NLP is the extension between respecting such individuals and having the option to show their conduct. It gives you a particular arrangement of techniques to have the option to copy the conduct essential to display their prosperity. It enables you to imitate greatness. Brain science's center is normal execution; neuro-linguistic programming's attention is on greatness.

In its center action, NLP is the displaying of greatness. At the outset, this appears as oblivious digestion and mirroring the conduct of the virtuoso until you can create from your conduct indistinguishable reactions from the virtuoso. Until you accomplish those criteria, you are staying lethargic and imitative. When you have accomplished that conduct, at that point, you really proceed onward to investigating what you are really doing and why it works.

Since demonstrating is so pivotal in neuro phonetic programming, it would bode well that you should discover somebody who accomplished something effectively and duplicate what they did to accomplish a specific objective that you have. This enables individuals to roll out significant improvements in their lives rapidly. Numerous very fruitful individuals have utilized it adequately. Present-day business preparing courses use it broadly, regardless of whether they don't give NLP express kudos for the ideas being instructed at the workshops. Additionally, numerous fruitful self-improvement masters, for example, Tony Robbins, utilize NLP to support workshop and preparing camp participants to accomplish significant changes in their lives in brief timeframes.

A specialist NLP professional can have the impact of rapidly affecting the conduct of someone else to transform them in manners they didn't think is conceivable. For instance, Tony Robbins and Richard Bandler are known for having the option to dispose of since a long time ago held fears that individuals have had in minutes. This is only one of the numerous ways that neuro phonetic programming can be effectively applied to improve our lives.

This concise NLP instructional exercise secured the focal point of neurolinguistic programming, yet it is an immense subject that manages greatness in different fields of the human undertaking, so there is a long way to go. Ideally, this sparked your interest, so you seek more data about this genuinely significant region that has profited numerous individuals' lives to improve things.

CHAPTER TEN

CONCLUSION

NLP is an amazing strategy dependent on the intensity of your psyche. Some may call it 'mind stunts' in any case, by utilizing these systems and others created by NLP professionals, you can figure out how to assume responsibility for your brain and how you react to the world.

NLP works from the beginning stage that you may not control much in your life, however, that you can generally assume responsibility for what goes on in your mind. Your contemplations, sentiments, and feelings are not things that are, or that you have, yet things that you do. Their causes can frequently be extremely confounded, including, for example, remarks or convictions from your folks or instructors, or occasions that you have encountered.

NLP gives you how you can assume responsibility for these convictions and impacts. Utilizing mind systems, for example, perception, you can change how you ponder past occasions, fears, and even fears.

It tries to respond to addresses that have a generally "oblivious" structure, those regularly in regards to convictions, knowing, and doing.

One of the first expectations supporting the advancement of NLP was the capacity to demonstrate conduct. On and when two individuals of equivalent physical and mental limit both endeavored to achieve something, and one was more fruitful than the other, at that point, what affected? Generally, it was the oblivious skill of one individual to perform superior to the next through the state (passionate and mental) the executives.

Right now, truly a great many pages have been composed depicting NLP and its different models and methods. Different characters, for example, Anthony Robbins, Robert Dilts, and Steve Andreas, have ascended to notoriety in light of NLP. Be that as it may, maybe above all, NLP is a model for change. At the point when applied by the individual or an equipped NLP professional, mental methodologies, language designs, physiology, attitude, passionate states, convictions, and qualities all move to get consistent with the ideal state and ultimate result. NLP uses an example that hinders to actually change the structure of neural pathways in the cerebrum – basically overhauling the educated conduct of the person.

Contrasted with psychoanalytic sorts of psychotherapy which empower an increasingly open-finished self-investigation, subjective conduct treatment is frequently most appropriate for customers who are progressively OK with an organized and centered methodology in which the advisor regularly plays an instructional job. Be that as it may, for CBT to be powerful, the individual must be prepared and ready to invest energy and exertion, breaking down their musings and emotions. Such self-investigation and schoolwork can be troublesome; however, it is an incredible method to become familiar with how inward states sway outward conduct.

Psychological conduct treatment is additionally appropriate for individuals searching for a transient treatment alternative for specific kinds of passionate trouble that doesn't really include psychotropic medicine. Probably the best advantage of psychological conduct treatment is that it assists customers with creating adapting aptitudes that can be helpful both now and later on.

Embedded headings are questions that lead with a suggestion of thought or imagined that by then becomes planted in the group of a spectators individual's mind. A request that starts with "What may it be like..." makes the crowd picture their answer before vocalizing it. Giving a thought setting makes it a reality, and by representing these sorts of requests, you are giving your group of spectators another reality and changing their conviction system.

Neuro-Linguistic Programming (NLP) looks at the pinions inside the machine that is the human personality; it causes us to comprehend what drives human conduct. It centers around how our contemplations, activities, feelings, and various other individual attributes cooperate to influence how we act.

Disregarding the way that NLP could be seen as a preparation that is used for control and control, it should be used as a positive effect for you and your general environment. Right when used importantly, NLP can firmly change your reality and reality of others that you come into contact with consistently. This positive effect lessens struggle and sustains associations.

Displaying in NLP is the way toward receiving the practices, language, methodologies, and convictions of someone else or model to 'construct a model of what they do...we realize that our demonstrating has been effective when we can methodically get a similar conduct result as the individual, we have modeled.'[citation needed] The 'model' is then reduced to an example that can be educated to other people. The examples found were created after some time and adjusted for general correspondence and affecting change. Modeling isn't bound to treatment, however, it can be and is applied to a wide scope of human learning. Another part of demonstrating is understanding the examples of one's practices to 'model' the more fruitful pieces of oneself.

The most effortless approach to clarify how NLP creates such astonishing outcomes is that it is a basic, direct way to deal with correspondence and self-improvement. NLP viably works with the structure of how individuals hold their substances set up, regardless of whether it be a straightforward affiliation one can make with a specific melody or whole conviction frameworks about how they believe the world to be. The individuals who study NLP adapt immediately the devices and abilities they have to legitimately and intentionally change contemplations and practices.

There is one progressively basic component that directly affects the adequacy of NLP – practice. Similarly, as with whatever else, NLP procedures must be drilled and utilized consistently for them to be best. Numerous individuals go to workshops or classes to find out about NLP, and that is the place they realize what they have to know. The genuine work and genuine development start when members head retreat into the world and spotlight on applying what they have realized in their regular day to day existence.

NLP is a prominent and successful way to deal with self-awareness and advancement. It is useful and conduct-based, which makes it moderately easy to instruct and incorporate. The methods can be utilized by any individual who knows them as a useful asset for improving lives.